HOW FANTASY SPORTS EXPLAINS THE WORLD

WHAT PUJOLS AND PEYTON CAN TEACH US ABOUT WOOKIEES AND WALL STREET

AJ MASS

Foreword by Matthew Berry

SKYHORSE PUBLISHING

Skyhorse Publishing books may be purchased in bulk at special discounts for sales promotion, corporate gifts, fund-raising, or educational purposes. Special editions can also be created to specifications. For details, contact the Special Sales Department, Skyhorse Publishing, 307 West 36th Street, 11th Floor, New York, NY 10018 or info@skyhorsepublishing.com.

Skyhorse® and Skyhorse Publishing® are registered trademarks of Skyhorse Publishing, Inc.®, a Delaware corporation.

www.skyhorsepublishing.com

10 9 8 7 6 5 4 3 2 1

Library of Congress Cataloging-in-Publication Data is available on file.

ISBN: 978-1-62087-603-9

Printed in the United States of America

FOR ANDREW KALANI LAMAR

CONTENTS

FOREWORD

I T BEGINS—AS MOST stories do—with a papier-mâché fish head.
I first met AJ Mass over twenty years ago at Syracuse University, where my friends and I were working at the student TV station. We had come up with the idea of doing a sitcom about a low-rent children's show host.

The host had a sidekick named Marty the Fishboy who was never to be seen. The joke was that we would describe all these horrific, ridiculous things our host made the Fishboy do—but they would never be onscreen. What's the old saying? Fishboys are meant to be seen, not heard? Wait. Heard, not seen. No, not seen or heard? Gimme a sec, I'll figure it out. The important part here is there wasn't ever supposed to be an actual Fishboy.

And what happened next would turn out to be a huge turning point in our lives, the world of fantasy sports and the art of papier-mâché.

You see, our prop person read the script quickly and didn't understand that the Fish, as we affectionately called him, was an off-screen character—the key word there being "off."

So imagine our shock at the next meeting when she showed up with an actual papier-mâché fish head. Actually, you don't have to imagine our shock; I'll tell you about it. We were shocked.

You should have seen this thing—large and bulky with bug eyes and painted-on scales. It was both ugly, hilarious, and completely impractical. What we should have done was to say, "Hey, prop girl Nicole, that's awesome, but we don't actually need it."

However, Nicole had spent a lot of time on it and more importantly was very attractive. So, being cowardly and stereotypically male, we of course immediately changed the whole concept of the show to have an actual person play the Fishboy.

AJ Mass was quickly chosen as the guy to play the well-thought-out and suddenly available role of Marty the Fishboy for two very crucial reasons: he fit the head and he was willing.

We ended up doing two years worth of shows. It won a bunch of student awards, and Marty the Fishboy became a fan favorite, earning a cultlike following. But most importantly, it started a friendship that continues to this day. A friendship that included, incidentally, AJ inviting me to play in my first-ever fantasy football league, a league that he was the commissioner of and one that is, as of this writing, in its eighteenth season.

I had played fantasy baseball for five years or so but had never done fantasy football at that point. And while I always loved fantasy baseball, fantasy football ignited a passion/obsession in me that, later in life, drove me to start writing about fantasy sports for a living—first on another site, then for my own Talented Mr. Roto site, and eventually for ESPN.

If I don't get invited into that league, who knows how my life turns out? And if Nicole doesn't show up with that fish head, who knows if I ever become friends with AJ to get invited into said league?

A story that starts with a papier-mâché fish head and ends with two guys making their living at fantasy sports writing isn't typical, but then again, neither is AJ Mass.

AJ looks at fantasy, and frankly life, in a way that is unique, to say the least. Even in the beginning, he always ran our league differently. From the scoring, to the rules, to the fun things he added on the side, ours was not a typical league in any way, shape, or form.

So when I started my own site in 2004, it was only natural that I asked AJ to write for it. AJ brought the same skewed vision of fantasy and the world to popular columns for my site and then, later, to ESPN and then even later (like as soon as you're done with this foreword) to this book. He has always provoked a strong reaction, the most important quality when looking for a writer.

You may not agree with everything in this book, but all of it will make you think. You'll question preconceived notions and ideas, you'll reevaluate strategy, and no matter if you are obsessed with fantasy sports, or you hate it because all your friends and lovers are obsessed with it, you'll look at it in an entirely different way. And not just in fantasy leagues, but how the same concepts you currently employ in fantasy can inform other parts of your life.

From how spending Christmas Eve with Allen Iverson can shed light on biases we use in our drafting of players to how the worst improvised show in history should be a guide when making a free-agent acquisition, AJ will entertain and challenge you every step of the way.

It's not often you see Darth Vader, Stephen Hawking, William Shakespeare, Jesus, economist Myron Scholes, Stan Van Gundy, Tuffy Rhodes, Abraham Lincoln's secretary of state, *Project Runway*, psychic Sylvia Browne, Monty Hall, Kanye West, the *Twilight* movies, Pai Gow Poker, Serbian inventor Nikola Tesla, and "Mr. Met" referenced in the same book, especially one about fantasy sports, but that's only because you haven't read a book by AJ Mass before.

This book will change your life. At least that's what AJ tells me. I haven't read the thing yet—I'm writing this off the outline he sent me. But you know what? Blind faith is a part of fantasy sports, so why shouldn't a foreword be? The crucial part is that you put this down, go to the register, and buy it.

Come on, you've read this far, you could at least plunk down a few bucks! You've definitely spent more money on worse, and by "you've" I really mean "I" and by "worse" I mean the money I spent on parking, popcorn, and two tickets to any M. Night Shyamalan movie after *The Sixth Sense*.

Seriously, I demand those hours of my life back—words you won't say after reading this book.

May all your sleepers pan out,
Matthew Berry, the Talented Mr. Roto
December 5, 2010

HOW FANTASY SPORTS
EXPLAINS THE WORLD

1

Christmas Eve with the Iversons

BEFORE I STARTED writing about fantasy sports for ESPN, I slapped the cards in Atlantic City as a professional dealer. Now, movies often make working in a casino seem glamorous, or at the very least fun. After all, who wouldn't want to be just like Wallace Shawn in *Vegas Vacation*, mocking Chevy Chase's every wager? Unfortunately, actually telling a customer, "You don't know when to quit, do ya, Griswold? Here's an idea: Why don't you give me half the money you were gonna bet, then we'll go out back, I'll kick you in the nuts, and we'll call it a day!" would likely be grounds for termination, even though every dealer has wanted to say something like that to at least one nuisance over the years.

While the perception may well be that dealers are experts in the games they deal, and love nothing more than "winning" each and every hand, generally speaking, that couldn't be further from the truth. First of all, becoming a dealer at an Atlantic City casino is not that difficult an accomplishment to achieve. All you have to do is take a course at a local dealing school or community college that teaches you the basic procedures of chip handling and game protection and then two game-specific classes out of blackjack, roulette, baccarat, or craps, just so you know where to stand and where the cards/dice/chips go. Then you go around to all the employment offices and see which ones happen to be hiring that day.

They'll schedule you for an audition, and you'll deal on a live game for about five to ten minutes. As long as you don't completely freeze, you'll probably get hired on the spot. Speaking English? Not really a prerequisite. An ability to do math? Definitely a plus, but not a deal breaker if you can't. Quite honestly, as long as you smile and make eye contact with the customers, you're in.

Why is the screening process so lax? Well, casinos know the odds are in their favor on every table game they offer. While there may be an isolated day where the gamblers come out ahead, over the course of a week or a month or a year, profit is all but guaranteed. Therefore, they're willing to take a hit on the odd erroneous payout on losing hands so long as the gambler is happy to stick around and gamble longer. Eventually, it all comes back to the house.

This is especially true in the "junk games" or "carnival games" as they're also called. Let it Ride, Caribbean Stud, and Three-Card Poker are just a few of the offerings in a casino that are so easy to deal, they'll happily stick a dealer on the game who has never even watched a single hand before. After all, the proper payouts are clearly printed on the green felt for all to see, and the house edge is so great that even with the occasional mistake made by the dealer, there's no fear of the table losing money so long as the player stays put in his or her seat long enough. However, an inexperienced dealer is a nervous dealer, and a nervous dealer is going to focus more on "getting it right" than conversing with the customers. So, when a high roller comes in—especially a notoriously abrasive one—the casino will usually opt for someone who doesn't rattle easily and, more importantly, a dealer who will be able to cope with the abuse long enough for the casino to make a killing.

And for this, an Atlantic City dealer makes around $4.25 per hour to start, with miniscule raises each calendar year, with a cap on earnings usually set around $8.00–$8.50 per hour, depending on the house. Yes, a twenty-five-year veteran dealer earns barely a dollar more than the legal minimum wage. How do the casinos get away with this? It's the tips, which are pooled by all the dealers after each business day and divided evenly. Unfortunately, these monies are not guaranteed, and the "toke rate"—the hourly average of tip money per dealer—can fluctuate wildly from week to week, making it difficult for a dealer to budget properly.

When the dealer wins, the customer loses, and when the customer loses, the customer doesn't tip. Which is why it's laughable to think the dealer is "out to get the gambler." The only time a dealer truly wants a customer to lose is after they've already had plenty of success at the table and proven themselves to be nontippers. At that point, the dealer may well use whatever limited influence they have—for example, by quickly dealing a card when the player makes a hand signal for a hit on a hand they should stick on before they have a chance to realize their mistake—to try and get that gambler's winnings back in the rack out of spite, but in the end, it still comes down to nothing more than luck.

That's one of the biggest differences between gambling in a casino and playing fantasy sports. While it certainly helps to know the odds of each possible wager to be made in the game you're playing, there's not a single one of them which is to the player's advantage. Combining this lack of control over the outcome with the "us versus them" mentality that many gamblers bring to the gaming tables and you've got the perfect recipe for frustration, outrage, and violent outbursts.

Compare that with fantasy sports, where you also have no real control over the performance of the players you've selected to play for your team. Once your lineups are set, you're simply a passive bystander, hoping for the result to fall in your favor. Just as after placing a bet on the roulette table, your only option is to watch the ball spin and hope the drop is favorable. The difference is that the evaluation of fantasy players is a skill that you can learn. Your knowledge of the game can, in fact, give you the edge over your opponent. While there's still an element of luck involved, you can decrease its impact, say, by drafting perennial top five fantasy running back Adrian Peterson of the Minnesota Vikings instead of

Adrian Peterson, the former running back for the Chicago Bears who couldn't even land a roster spot in 2010.

My first day on the job as a professional casino dealer, I dealt blackjack. My second day on the job, I dealt blackjack. My third day on the job, I dealt blackjack. In fact, for the first two weeks, I only dealt blackjack. On the one hand, after two weeks straight on the same game, I learned I could deal blackjack in my sleep. On the other hand, I very often did just that.

Good dealers, which I quickly learned was a group that included me, develop a kind of rhythm. You don't really see the cards or actually do the math—you simply get into a kind of trance, and you only snap out of it when that rhythm is disturbed, either by a mistaken payout which you simply "feel" or by a customer making some sort of unnatural movement or placing a wager that is outside of the norm. At this point, you "wake up" and assess the situation, make the necessary correction, and then return to your semicomatose state until you feel the tap on your left shoulder from your relief dealer signifying it is time for your next break.

Customers actually appreciate dealers who can achieve this sort of "Zen state" as it makes their lives easier as well. Many of them are putting in shifts at the blackjack table that go on twice as long as that of the dealer. When they have confidence that the dealer knows what they are doing, they'll relax as well and simply trust that you're dealing the game correctly. Many a time I would have a player question me and say something like, "Didn't I push that hand?" and without even thinking, I'd recall, "No, you had 18, I had 19." And because they could see I was on autopilot, they knew I was right, even if five seconds later I'd forgotten that hand entirely and moved on to the next one.

The reason for this comes down to the fact that blackjack is not a game of skill at all. At every moment where the player has a "decision" to make, there is an optimal choice, based on the rules of probability that is the best call. Now, that best choice may not win each and every time, but in the long run, you'll lose less often if you follow this basic strategy. Most experienced gamblers understand this and will always make the "right" call.

The better dealers also understand this and learn to expect the "right" call. When that's working in synergy, the game flows smoothly and at a pace that pleases both the casino (which stands to make more money the more hands that are dealt) as well as the gambler (who wants to play as many hands as possible to get that gambler's rush as many times as they can before their bankroll runs out.)

Unfortunately, far too often, a blackjack table will be hijacked by someone who fails to grasp the basic mathematics and the immutable probabilities of the game. These gamblers fall into two basic categories. One is the truly ignorant neophyte, who simply doesn't know what they are doing. That's at least excusable, though my sympathy for them usually would disappear quickly when they would ask for my advice on what to do, and then either decide to ignore it or get angry when the advice I gave them failed to work on a particular occasion.

It's the same thing in fantasy sports. I was asked in early September 2009 which pitcher I'd rather have for the rest of the regular season: Roy Halladay or CC Sabathia. I recommended Halladay, who then promptly allowed four earned runs and lost his next start. Meanwhile, Sabathia struck out ten batters and allowed only one earned run during his next trip to the mound.

The venomous posts on the ESPN message boards appeared quickly: "How did you get your job, AJ? You call yourself an expert? You're an idiot! You were wrong!"

I wasn't wrong, just as I would not be wrong to recommend that you hit your 13 with the dealer showing a face card. Sure, when you draw a 10 and bust, you lose the hand. That doesn't mean the advice was wrong. It just didn't work out this time. You can't judge the advice based on one hand of blackjack. Over the long haul, you'll win more than you lose by following basic blackjack strategy.

And over the long haul for the remainder of the 2009 season, Halladay had just as many wins as Sabathia, a better ERA, and more strikeouts. My advice certainly *could have* been wrong, but as it turned out, in this case it was not. One start from each pitcher was far too soon to pass judgment.

The other basic category of gambler who disrupts the flow of a blackjack table is what I like to call the PBS: psychic but stupid. These gamblers intently stare at the cards on the table, trying to use their "psychic abilities" to decide whether or not to hit a 16 against a dealer's face card. There's no trick here; you play the odds.

Unless you are a skilled card counter from MIT specially trained by Kevin Spacey, you are supposed to hit your 16 and not even hesitate to do so. Yes, you may bust, but over the long term, you will end up winning more often by hitting than by standing pat. And yet, nearly every day, this situation would arise at a table, and the player would hem and haw and try to look for some sort of sign from the heavens as to what to do.

Inevitably, this is how it plays out: the player will stand on 16, since the odds of them getting a 6 or higher (thus breaking) is 62 percent, greater than the chances of drawing a 5 or lower. (The reason this logic is flawed is that with a face card showing the dealer already has a 58 percent chance of having a "made hand" that already has them beat.)

Anyway, after the game has screeched to a halt waiting for the table's resident Miss Cleo to divine the proper course of action and she finally stands on 16, the next player hits and a 5 comes out of the shoe.

"I knew it! I knew it!" she says.

Sure you did, Cleo. After all you're psychic, right? Psychic and stupid—since you "knew it" and yet decided not to hit. Please! You didn't know it. You just guessed wrong during a situation where guessing has no value.

These are the same people who bench a superstar quarterback like Peyton Manning when he's facing the tough Pittsburgh Steelers defense in favor of an inferior quarterback like Jimmy Clausen, who's going up against the putrid Cleveland Browns. Yes, it might work out for you—there are no guarantees in fantasy football—but the odds are certainly not in your favor.

· · ·

Reverse Psychology

In the 1950s, long before the advent of the computer age, four men known collectively as "The Four Horsemen" figured out what has come to be known as "basic strategy" for playing blackjack. Their calculations, which have since been found to be nearly 100 percent accurate by modern computer simulations of millions of hands of blackjack, form the basis of the chart found below.

You can minimize the house's edge—and thus maximize your odds of winning—by following this chart to the letter, which tells you when to hit, stand, split pairs, and if it is wise to double down or not, all based on the upcard that the dealer is showing.

Of course, most casinos are happy to let you bring this card with you to the blackjack table and refer to it as often as you like. Why? Because although it does, in fact, maximize your odds, you're still only bound to win around 47 percent of the hands that aren't pushes. (Hands in which the dealer and player end up with the same total are called "pushes." The bet remains on the table. Nobody wins and nobody loses.)

Additionally, the casinos are banking on reverse psychology to cause you to doubt the accuracy of this mathematically sound strategy. Many a skeptical gambler has been heard to say, "If the casino will let me use this card, it must favor the casino."

It's the same kind of strategy a savvy fantasy owner will utilize on draft day, talking up a player they have no intention of drafting themselves, hoping that someone less confident in their own ability to evaluate talent will "steal" this player out from under them, leaving a more desirable pick behind for the snickering owner to snatch for himself.

In both situations, you've got to be able to stick to your guns and do what you know is right, no matter what doubts seep in as a result of the unsolicited advice of the people around you.

Basic Strategy

4 - 8 Decks, Dealer stands soft 17, Double after split

Dealer's up-card

	2	3	4	5	6	7	8	9	10	A
5-8	H	H	H	H	H	H	H	H	H	H
9	H	D	D	D	D	H	H	H	H	H
10	D	D	D	D	D	D	D	D	H	H
11	D	D	D	D	D	D	D	D	D	H
12	H	H	S	S	S	H	H	H	H	H
13	S	S	S	S	S	H	H	H	H	H
14	S	S	S	S	S	H	H	H	H	H
15	S	S	S	S	S	H	H	H	SR	H
16	S	S	S	S	S	H	H	SR	SR	SR
A2	H	H	H	D	D	H	H	H	H	H
A3	H	H	H	D	D	H	H	H	H	H
A4	H	H	D	D	D	H	H	H	H	H
A5	H	H	D	D	D	H	H	H	H	H
A6	H	D	D	D	D	H	H	H	H	H
A7	S	D/S	D/S	D/S	D/S	S	S	H	H	H
2-2	P	P	P	P	P	P	H	H	H	H
3-3	P	P	P	P	P	P	H	H	H	H
4-4	H	H	H	P	P	H	H	H	H	H
6-6	P	P	P	P	P	H	H	H	H	H
7-7	P	P	P	P	P	P	H	H	H	H
8-8	P	P	P	P	P	P	P	P	P	P
9-9	P	P	P	P	P	S	P	P	S	S

Player's hand (row label)

Key:

H	Hit
S	Stand
D	Double down / else Hit
P	Split
SR	Surrender / else Hit
D/S	Double down / else Stand

Additional Basic Strategy:
1) Never take insurance
2) Always stand hard 17 or higher
3) Always stand A8, A9, A10, and 10-10
4) Always play 5-5 as a 10
5) Always split Aces

T HE FACT IS that not only are the perks of the casino dealer's job few and far between, there are also actually a litany of "antiperks" that make the job all the more difficult to remain upbeat and positive about. For one, your schedule can change on a whim. You'll have an assigned shift: either day, swing, or grave. But even within those designations, there can be plenty of fluctuation. For example, "day shift" might mean 6:00 AM–2:00 PM, 10:00 AM–6:00 PM, noon–8:00 PM, or even 2:00 PM–10:00 PM, and you won't know until the previous week for what times you'll be scheduled.

In fact, while you generally—although not always—get two consecutive days off each week, they're not guaranteed to be on the same two days each week—and all but assuredly will not involve any weekend time off. Holidays? Forget about it. You're working on Christmas, New Year's Eve, Thanksgiving, Presidents Day, Halloween, Arbor Day, Purim, you name it. The casino never closes, so somebody—and that "somebody" most likely includes you—always has to work.

Which leads us to December 24, 2003. I reported to work at Bally's as scheduled at 11:45 AM and checked *The Daily*, which would let us know which specific table to report to, and saw I was likely in for a very long, very dull day. Usually, the day shift at a casino has a steady supply of gamblers, most of which consists of senior citizens who have taken the bus down the Garden State Parkway from the Big Apple to spend their mad money either at the slot machines or at low-limit gaming tables.

Christmas Eve was a different animal, however. Most people tended to stay at home—preparing for the holiday festivities of the evening to come. We always expected a heavier-than-usual crowd of Asians who, generally speaking, don't have any cultural history of either celebrating Jesus's birthday or dressing up in red and white and saying, "Ho, ho, ho!" However, the Asians tended to gravitate toward games such as Baccarat, Mini-Baccarat, Pai Gow Poker, and Sic Bo.

As for me, I was scheduled to man the Big Six. This is the worst spot in the casino, and the computer-generated schedule had given me the short straw. You're by yourself, standing in front of a giant spoked wheel that would make Pat Sajak green with envy. On it are pictures of different denominations of currency. Players can place a $1 chip on the glass table in front of them, selecting the denomination of their choice; and if the wheel stops on that value, they win that amount. If not, they lose.

Brain surgery it isn't, but unfortunately, due to the fact it is one of the only games in the casino you can play for a single dollar, it can draw a huge crowd that never thins out. Most of the folks attracted to this game have little to no gambling experience, but at the asking price, they typically play the game just to be able to cross "gamble at a casino" off their personal bucket list. Of course, few of these kinds of people grasp the fact that the reason George Washington happens to come up far more than, say, the more lucrative Andrew Jackson, is not because the game is "rigged" or that the dealer spinning the wheel is "cheating" but for the far more mundane reason that there are simply more pictures of our first president on the wheel.

Eventually, though, even the densest of minds catches on, and they begin to grasp that this game has some of the worst odds for the gambler in the entire casino, as well as the lowest payouts. Once that genie is out of the bottle, you may well spend the rest of your shift without a single customer bothering to come your way. In short, it's a case of feast or famine, and either way you end up wanting to shoot yourself by the time your shift is over.

· · ·

Understanding the Odds

Let's take a closer look at why Big Six is such a lousy game for the gambler. On the surface, a payout of $20 for placing a $1 chip on the "20 spot" on the table may seem like a good deal, until you actually do the math. There are fifty-four slots on the wheel, and only two of them are 20s. Therefore, your expected winnings per wager are as follows:

$$(52/54)*(-\$1) + (2/54)*(\$20) = (0.963)*(-\$1) + (0.037)*(\$20) = (-0.963) + (0.74) = -22.3\%$$

That's not exactly screaming out for you to place that money down. Even the "safe bet" of going for even money will yield a house edge of almost 15 percent. In short, much like Matthew Broderick taught the computer Joshua about Global-Thermo Nuclear War in *WarGames*, the only winning move is not to play.

A real-life example of why one should always make sure he knows the odds before agreeing to a wager occurred back in 1969. Ken Harrelson was traded from the Boston Red Sox to the Cleveland Indians a few games into the season, and at first, he decided to retire rather than accept the deal. Ultimately, he did agree to a two-year deal and reported to the Indians. However, as one story goes, though probably apocryphal, during negotiations with Cleveland General Manager Gabe Paul, Harrelson agreed to play the rest of the season without a salary—except for 50 cents, which would double for every home run he hit.

In other words, if he hit one home run, he'd make 50 cents. Two homers would earn him $1. Three home runs would net him $2 and so on. So, would you make this deal if you were Paul?

If you said yes, you are in a heap of trouble. Harrelson hit 27 home runs for the Indians that season, which at the rate of increase that he had requested would have been worth $33,554,432, about 280 times the salary future Hall of Famer Willie Mays was making that season for the San Francisco Giants. Let that serve as a reminder that if you're not sure of the math involved, just politely decline and tiptoe away.

I THOUGHT I GOT my reprieve when my reputation earned me a special assignment from Richard, my pit boss. I was to deal Three Card Poker to Allen Iverson and his family. Boy was I ever wrong.

The first thing you notice about Allen Iverson in person is his impressive size. On the basketball court, he appears so small, but that is an illusion. Iverson is listed as being an even six feet tall, and perhaps that's generous. But if you took the press guide at its word, this still made him the shortest member of the Philadelphia 76ers by a good four inches. Considering that there were many NBA players at the time who were seven feet or taller, Iverson was frequently dwarfed on the basketball court by men over a foot taller than he.

Sitting at the Three Card Poker table, however, he was a sight to behold. His hair was pulled back in his trademark cornrows, with a sideways baseball cap atop his head. Even wearing baggy sweats, you could see how chiseled his physique was. Make no mistake, this was a professional athlete. And after a brief chat with the casino host, who was there to cater to his every whim, he was ready to gamble. Before too long he was doing so with such gusto that I feared for my safety.

"Gimme my fucking money!"

His fist pounded down on the table with such force that I recoiled as though I myself had been struck by the blow. He rose from his chair, and his voice grew louder still, the alcohol on his breath just as capable of choking me to death even if his hands remained at his sides, which of course they did not.

"That's right, bitch! Gimme my fucking money!"

Again he pounded the table. An evil, self-satisfied chuckle sprung from his lips as I very carefully placed the $600 in question in front of him.

"Deal the cards, motherfucker! Let's go. Don't stop now. I'm on a roll!"

I finished collecting the cards from the table and placed them in the Shuffle Master automatic shuffling machine, then proceeded to dole out the cards for the next round of play.

Allen Iverson rubbed his hands together in gleeful anticipation.

"Here we go!"

Here's the thing about a game like Three Card Poker, though: there is no active participation from the gambler to be found. For those unfamiliar with the game, which bears little resemblance to real poker, here are the basic rules. The player places a bet on the table to get his cards. After looking at his hand, the player can either fold, forfeiting the bet, or place a second bet equal in value to the original wager to stay in the hand. After all the players have made their decision, the dealer reveals the three cards in front of him.

If the dealer's hand isn't at least "queen high" then the hand is immediately declared null and void. All players who folded still lose, but those who stayed in the hand effectively "push." If the dealer qualifies for play, then the hands are compared and the higher hands win. A player earns even money on each winning bet. Hands that are a straight, three of a kind, or a straight flush also receive a small bonus payout.

There is also a second "side wager" that has nothing to do with the dealer's hand. Before the cards are dealt, players may place a "pair plus" bet, which pays out, as the name indicates, on all hands of a pair or better. With a 40-to-1 payout on a three-card straight flush, this can be an exciting payoff for the gambler; but considering the fact that nearly three out of every four hands results in a losing pair plus wager, it's hardly worth it in the long run, despite the excitement of a few large hits.

Essentially, it boils down to this: you play the pair plus and then fold any hand that is worse than queen-seven. That's it. You don't have any real decision to make. You simply look at the cards and see what you have. There's no bluffing involved. You can't, as on a regular poker table, turn a "seven high" into a winning hand simply by posturing and using psychology to convince your opponent into believing you have a better hand than he does and causing him to fold. A "seven high" is a push at best (if the dealer doesn't qualify), and more than likely a loser. You let it go.

· · ·

Who's in Control Here?

When you're playing a game like Three Card Poker, where you really have no decisions to make—you either have a higher hand than the dealer or you don't—ultimately you have no control over the outcome. The same holds true for fantasy sports. Sure, you have a chance to set your own lineups and select the athletes you believe give you the best chance of winning, but once the games themselves begin, you become simply a spectator, hoping for the best.

However, sometimes the players themselves are not truly in control of their actions. Case in point: Maurice Jones-Drew of the Jacksonville Jaguars, who was on his way to the end zone for an uncontested touchdown in Week 11 of the 2009 season against the New York Jets, when he suddenly dropped to one knee at the 1-yard line so that his team could run out the clock before kicking a game-winning field goal. While the move made perfect sense in "real football," it created quite the uproar in fantasy circles.

In fact, by ESPN.com estimates, approximately ten thousand fantasy owners on their website lost that week's matchup because of Maurice Jones-Drew's action, including Maurice Jones-Drew himself. At a postgame press conference, Jones-Drew explained, "Sorry to my fantasy owners. I apologize. I had myself [starting in fantasy] today. It was a tough call, but whatever it takes to get the victory, that's what counts."

So why did he do it? Well, because he's a professional football player, and his coach told him to. That's why. If he had scored the touchdown against his coach's wishes, there would have been hell to pay. So, just like you, the fantasy owner, Maurice Jones-Drew really had no control over his performance on that play—much like a blackjack dealer at the casino who has no choice but to hit on 16 and stick on 17 (as the house dictates), regardless of his/her own personal wishes.

Sure, there's the rare occasion when an athlete takes it upon himself to do something completely unorthodox, like when a cleanup hitter in baseball drops down a bunt when he sees the third baseman is playing way too deep, but more often than not, the player's free will in determining the ultimate outcome of your fantasy game is exactly the same as yours—zero; the plays either get called for him, or they don't.

A S THE DAY wore on, I watched as AI imbibed a nonstop succession of Heineken and Hennessey, one following right after the other. He never once tipped any of the waitresses, and not a single one of them would return to serve him for a second time, due to the abusive language hurled in their direction by the table. And mind you, the other players at the table were members of Iverson's family! From right to left, there was his uncle George, a nameless pair of cousins, and then Iverson's mother herself seated next to him the whole time (but her baby could do no wrong in her eyes). She just sat there, massaging both the shoulder and knee that had been causing Iverson so much pain that he was unable to join the 76ers on their current road trip to the West Coast, which was why he was able to be at an Atlantic City casino in the midst of the NBA regular season.

As Iverson got noticeably drunker and drunker, he started to slur his speech. He also seemed to regress more and more into a childlike state. It was all I could do to keep from vomiting a little in my mouth as I listened to the following exchange between mother and son.

"Mama?"

"Yes, baby?"

"How on earth did you get so lucky to have given birth to a man such as me?"

"I am blessed."

"You *are* blessed."

Now certainly, after several hours of playing, news that a celebrity of Allen Iverson's stature was playing at this particular table had spread throughout the casino. It was bound to have happened. Iverson certainly had come prepared, as he had three guys standing behind the table, making sure that nobody dared approach him for an autograph. And if somebody simply wanted to be a spectator to a few hands, and stood for just a little too long, they, shall we say, "politely requested" that they move it along.

Of course, I say three guys because the same three guys were standing there for around five hours. As it turns out, guy number 3 wasn't part of the entourage. And for whatever reason, despite his having stood there watching pretty much since Iverson sat down at the table, and having not once opened his mouth to utter a single sound, his presence suddenly infuriated Iverson.

"What you looking at? What the fuck you looking at, motherfucker?"

Suddenly, Iverson rose to his feet and approached guy number 3 and got as close to him as humanly possible without actually making contact. A staredown ensued, and you just knew the slightest spark would send this powder keg sky high. Casino security, who had been standing nearby at the ready, quickly began to remove the offending individual from the scene to prevent any actual violence, but AI continued to scream and shout profanities after him as he was escorted away. He then turned his anger toward pit boss Richard.

"Why did you let him stand there so long? Why didn't you do something?"

Richard answered honestly, "We thought he was with you."

The whole table exploded, throwing their arms in the air. Iverson decided to turn this into a racial incident, saying, "You think that just because he was black, that means he's with me? Because I'm black? Let me tell you something . . ."

Uncle George turned to me and started pleading his case, "See, that's what always happens to AI. He got this reputation for being a bad guy. But he never starts anything. That guy started it by hanging 'round where he didn't belong, and your boss didn't do nothing to stop it. AI didn't start nothing. He had to defend himself, but it always gets turned around."

Richard tried to respond. "He was standing there for *hours*," he said. "If you had said something, we'd have asked him to go. You didn't say anything."

"Fuck you!"

"OK, knock off the cursing. Why don't you have a seat, slow down on the drinks for a while, and calm down."

"Calm down? I'm a grown man. I can drink. I can smoke. I can cuss. I'm a grown man. I can do what I want, motherfucker."

Eventually, Allen's mother got him to sit down; and before too long, he was out cold, snoring away at the table. Normally, that's a no-no. However, in this case, we let it slide, happy for the brief respite from the table pounding and the cursing. And then, a funny thing happened. No longer under the surveillance of AI, Mrs. Iverson and Uncle George, and even his cousins, started tipping me for the first time all day. It was as if they were tacitly apologizing for his behavior, now that he was in no position to see them make such an apology.

The final hour of my Christmas Eve with Iverson was, at long last, a joyous time, as Allen slept in heavenly peace…

People who play fantasy sports are always looking for an edge— that one hidden piece of wisdom that everyone else has ignored—in order to boost their chances of finishing on top of the heap. The fact is that these hidden nuggets of wisdom are all around us—in classic works of literature, in our legal and political systems, in the very molecules that make up the air we breathe. If we choose to do so, we can take lessons away from each and every situation we encounter and apply them to fantasy sports—and vice versa.

Do you enjoy that cell phone you talk into every day? Well, it might not exist—at least not in its current form—if not for the fact that its inventor, Martin Cooper, watched *Star Trek* and wanted to make a real-life communicator. Inspiration can come from anywhere, and that holds true for advances in technology, for political revolutions, and yes, even for innovative fantasy sports strategy.

•   •   •

Don't Mess with Captain Kirk

Whether you're in a casino, or joining a fantasy sports league, you should never play a game when you don't fully understand the rules going in. This is as true today as it will be in the future, when Captain James T. Kirk of the *Starship Enterprise* escapes from an alien captor by inviting him to play a card game known as Fizzbin. While Kirk explains the game as being popular on the planet Beta Antares IV, it's clear that the only place this game exists is in Kirk's head, and he's creating the rules as he's going along.

Some highlights of Kirk's improvisational ramblings:

- Each player gets six cards, except for the player on the dealer's right, who gets seven.

- The second card is turned up, except on Tuesdays.

- Two jacks are a "half-fizzbin" but a third jack is a "shralk" and results in disqualification.

- With a "half-fizzbin," you need a king and a deuce to win, except at night, when a queen and a four are the required cards to make your hand.

- If a king is dealt, the player does get another card, except when it is dark, in which case he'd have to give it back.

Got it? Neither does the alien, who didn't even pick up on the fact that the third card Kirk deals him is a jack, which should result in a "shralk" and a disqualification according to the captain's recitation of the rules. And yet, Kirk says, "How lucky you are! How wonderful for you!" Eventually, Kirk "accidentally" drops a card, and when the alien bends over to pick it up, he's met with a Vulcan nerve pinch from Mr. Spock, and the crew safely beams back to their ship.

What can we learn from this cautionary tale? Don't sit down at a poker table if you don't know the ranks of the hands. Don't join a fantasy baseball league if you don't know what WHIP means (for the record, it means *walks* plus *hits* divided by *innings pitched*). Learn the rules and the terminology in advance, and only then venture into the action. Otherwise, you've already lost.

When will humanoids learn?

W HAT DID I learn from my encounter with Allen Iverson? One, it reinforced my understanding that if you want to succeed at fantasy sports, you have to eliminate your personal feelings about players when you go to decide whom you want to draft for your team.

My personal dislike for Iverson—not only from his actions that day, but also from the stories I'd heard about the rest of his stay at Bally's—knew no bounds. A craps dealer told me that Iverson was playing at his table and making fun of his being a tad overweight. The dealer happened to be a season-ticket holder for the 76ers and told Iverson so. "You shouldn't make fun of your fans," the dealer said. "We help pay your salary." The alleged response? "That's a nice thought. Now have another sandwich."

Richard told me he was so shocked by what he had witnessed that day, he went home and had his young son burn his Iverson jersey in the fireplace. He was no longer allowed to root for him while living under his roof. Eventually, even the powers that be at Bally's had had their fill of AI when, in February of 2004, he decided that the bathroom was too far to walk; and he urinated in the vicinity of a trash can on the casino floor, resulting in his being permanently banned from the premises.

However, all that aside, people who play fantasy sports don't actually have to hang out with these athletes. We don't invite them over to meet our parents. We draft them for the statistics they produce, not for their personalities. We play with numbers, not names. And so, while I will never forget that Allen Iverson was an All-Star jerk, so long as he continued to be an All-Star talent, I'd still want him on my fantasy team.

Let's say I did hold a grudge against Iverson for his actions that day when I drafted my fantasy basketball team for the 2004 season and passed on taking him in the first round. What an idiot I would have been! All Iverson did that season was lead the league in points per game (30.7), steals (180) and free throws made (656). He also finished third in the NBA in assists with 596. He was a first-team All-NBA player who ended up finishing fifth in the MVP Voting that season, making him a fantasy basketball juggernaut.

I may not always like the players I draft, but if I want to win, I can't let that stop me from having them on my team. Maybe you're very fond of animals. Perhaps you're even a member of PETA. But if you decided to pass on Michael Vick in 2010 simply because of his well-documented involvement in illegal dog fighting and his subsequent incarceration, and chose instead to draft rookie Tim Tebow, who spent his college summers doing missionary work at an orphanage in the Philippines instead of lounging on the sunny beaches of Florida, then you were really just shooting yourself in the foot.

Vick ended up as the highest-scoring quarterback in ESPN leagues, with 300 fantasy points, while Tebow—although he led the league in jersey sales—finished well back of the pack at his position, tied for twenty-ninth place, with only 95 fantasy points to his highly regarded name.

And the reverse also holds true. For four seasons in the 1990s, I worked for the New York Mets as Mr. Met, the team mascot—the stories from my experiences there could fill a book of their own—and when people ask me which player with whom I had the most favorable personal experience, without hesitation I answer Carl Everett, a response that usually elicits quite a bit of surprise.

Everett's reputation as a player was that of a hothead who frequently got into arguments with teammates, managers, and umpires over the course of his career. One memorable explosion came when he was with the Boston Red Sox. Everett, who stands very close to the plate when he hits, was cautioned by home plate umpire Ron Kulpa to step back a bit. The resulting argument ended up with Everett being restrained by teammates and suspended for ten games after headbutting Kulpa in anger.

Everett's image didn't get any help in April of 2011, when he was charged with aggravated assault with a deadly weapon after allegedly putting a handgun to his wife's head during an argument at his Tampa Bay home.

Most baseball fans, when hearing his name, either think about those incidents, or they chuckle to themselves about Everett's outspoken views that dinosaurs didn't exist and that the Apollo moon landing was faked. Still, I never met a baseball player who, on a day-to-day basis, was nicer, more interested in what my job entailed, and genuinely thankful for the extra attention I gave to his kids if they crossed my path in the "back of house" parts of Shea Stadium.

But even though I liked Carl Everett, it would have been silly for me to continue to draft him for my fantasy team when there were many other outfielders available for selection whose stats dwarfed his own. In his final season in Boston, in 2001, he hit only .257 with 14 home runs and 58 RBIs in 102 games. The next season, a fresh start in Texas brought only a slight increase in production:

.267 with 16 home runs and 62 RBIs in 105 games. The rest of his career saw him shipped around the league from organization to organization—Montreal, Chicago (White Sox), and Seattle.

The same would be true of drafting a player because he once signed an autograph for you, was genuinely nice when you asked him to pose for a picture with your kid, or perhaps even donated tons of money to a charity you believe in. Those are certainly reasons to admire said player, but it doesn't suddenly transform a third-string running back into Walter Payton.

In fact, to be fair to Allen Iverson, less than a year after my encounter with him in Atlantic City, he was honored by the NBA with their Community Assist Award for his work with Boys & Girls Clubs, as well as the Make-a-Wish Foundation, and several other charities that he supports year-round. If that was the only experience I had with Iverson, perhaps the glasses through which I view him as a person would be far more rose colored, but my evaluation of him for fantasy purposes would not change a bit.

Statistics and probabilities have made athletes like Allen Iverson rich and have also allowed fans to feel a level of participation beyond that of a simple spectator through the fantasy sports games they play. And it's that same kind of attention to mathematics that would have served Iverson well at the casino, if only he'd cared to learn.

2

WWJD: Who Would Jesus Draft?

SOMETHING IN YOUR fantasy league isn't working. You used to have a lot of fun playing fantasy sports, but now you look forward to draft day about as much as a trip to the dentist. Arguments between owners spring up at the drop of a hat, and suggestions you offer to make things better are met with hems and haws as your fellow owners refuse to go along with anything that might challenge the status quo. And, in the words of Dr. Horrible, the status is definitely not quo.

What went wrong? Well, every group has a better chance of survival if it has a nice mix of personality types in its ranks. If your fantasy league has a whole bunch of argumentative "have to be right all the time" headstrong owners and not enough peace-making, level-headed "let's try to reach a compromise" types, it is doomed to repeat this cycle: season begins, headaches begin, yelling begins, bad feelings stew, full-on league brouhaha develops, owners mutiny, season is ruined, season mercifully ends.

But before we get into figuring out the best recipe of personalities to ensure your league's longevity, we need to understand that, to put it bluntly, size matters. Too few owners and you end up with rosters full of nothing but superstars. The waiver wires are always full of easy-to-find replacement studs as well, so in essence, all of the skill is taken out of the equation. In leagues like that, owners realize quickly there's little they can do to influence their team's success. Over time it becomes more and more of a passive exercise, and it's very easy for owners to lose interest.

On the other end of the spectrum, if your league has too many teams, there may not even be enough starting players to go around. One injury can completely cripple an owner's chances of winning, especially with nothing left on the waiver wire except practice squad fodder. If you have Tony Romo as your quarterback and he goes down—as he did in 2010—there's no way you can win your league if your only options for a free agent pickup force you to choose between Brett Basanez and Thaddeus Lewis. Even the most hardcore of football fans have likely never heard of those guys. Why should anyone be surprised when Romo's owner decides to check out?

But how many owners are too few? When do you have too many cooks in the proverbial kitchen? What's the answer? Perhaps we should turn to a higher power for help.

There's something magical about the number 12. From a mathematical standpoint, 12 is one of only two numbers that are considered to be "sublime"—a word that means "having outstanding spiritual, intellectual, or moral worth." Without delving too much into the world of number theory, let's just say that a sublime number (one that has a "perfect number of divisors" as well as the sum of those divisors also being "perfect") is extremely rare. (The only other known sublime number is the unwieldy 6086555670238 37898967037173424316962265783077335188597052832486 0512791691264. Suffice it to say that's probably a few too many owners for even the most ambitious of leagues to consider.)

Even without understanding the calculus involved, it's clear that throughout all of human history, the number 12 has always had a revered place. Not only do our clocks go to twelve, but there are twelve months in our calendar and twelve signs of the zodiac. We sell some of our most basic nutritional needs, eggs and baked goods, in dozens.

American criminal juries have twelve members in deliberations, and King Arthur had twelve knights in his Round Table.

When Lee Marvin needed to get down and dirty to battle the Nazis, you know how many men he chose to do the job? That's right—twelve.

When it comes to religion, there may be a lot of differences in the names and places and many of the "rules," but yet that number 12 always seems to pop up. Be it the twelve members in the council of Dalai Lama, the twelve gods and goddesses of Mount Olympus, the twelve descendants of Ali in Islam, the twelve tribes of Israel, or the twelve followers of the Zoroastrian deity, Mithra (not to be confused with the giant Godzilla-fighting winged insect, Mothra, who had a far greater number of followers, including two diminutive Japanese songstresses)—it's not just Christianity that has exclusive rights over the number 12.

Now when it comes to fantasy football, it's pretty clear to me that 12 is the ideal number of owners to have. For one thing, you can divide teams evenly into three divisions of four teams each which, combined with the current seventeen-week NFL schedule, allows you to play every owner in your division twice, every other owner once, and still have enough time to schedule a playoff to determine your league champion.

Not only that, but when the NFL inevitably goes to an eighteen-game schedule for each team, a quick switch to two six-team divisions will work out just fine in increasing your own schedule by two games in a fair and balanced way without the need to add new franchises to the mix.

Plus, with thirty-two NFL teams, having twelve fantasy squads allows you to have enough good players at each position to go around while also leaving enough undrafted talent with which teams can make any necessary roster moves during the season.

But what about Jesus? Was there a particular reason he opted to have twelve apostles rather than any other number? It certainly couldn't have been just so they would all fit into the picture when Leonardo da Vinci came over to paint their portrait over dinner.

Now, before I answer that question, a confession. Most of what I know about Catholicism comes from reading Dan Brown novels. I don't consider myself to be religious at all. I think it's nigh on impossible for any child who was raised in a mixed-faith family, as I was, to truly buy in to any organized faith. My mother is an Irish Catholic and my father is Jewish. As a result of some sort of bizarre compromise, my parents decided to send me to the nearest church in order to enrich my spiritual education.

· · ·

No Novel Ideas Here

In fantasy sports, when a player puts up the same stat line year in and year out, he's what we call reliable. Fantasy owners love being able to draft guys like Bobby Abreu or Nene Hilario and be confident that they'll produce exactly as expected, with no surprises.

While predictability is a huge plus in fantasy sports, that's not the case when it comes to thriller fiction intended to shock and surprise the reader. Case in point, when I read Dan Brown's latest novel, I was very disappointed. I'm afraid that Brown, whose previous books I've enjoyed, has become way too formulaic. There was simply nothing fresh or surprising in *The Lost Symbol*. The story falls back on too many of the same clichés that drove the plots of *Angels and Demons* and *The DaVinci Code*.

I won't spoil the plot, for those of you still planning to read *The Lost Symbol*, but to prove my point, I will now help Brown out by writing the plot of his next novel for him. Here it is, hot off the presses: *The Forgotten King*.

Robert Langdon gets a call waking him in the middle of the night. He needs to come to the campus of Texas A&M immediately. As so often happens in real life, there's been an incident that only a symbologist can assist with.

Reluctantly, he arrives at the school where he learns that the school's mascot, a dog named Reveille, has been murdered and covered with what appear to be ancient Egyptian hieroglyphs, in the shape of a serpent. Langdon is also given a tour of the school by a single female grad student who has studied abroad and recounts for him some of the outlandish and unsubstantiated rumors about the school—that some believe it to be part of grand conspiracy, due to its connections to NASA, cloning, and George W. Bush.

Meanwhile, in the shadows, one of the cadets, a man with a bizarre physical deformity to be determined, watches from a distance, swearing that he will kill Langdon if he gets too close to the truth.

Langdon suddenly has a revelation while looking at a picture of Wen Ho Lee on the alumni wall and realizes the hieroglyphs stand for "misunderstood spy." Obviously, this points to an anagram. And when Langdon figures out the anagram, he is stunned at what he discovers. But before he can inform the reader, shots ring out, and Langdon and his tour guide are forced to flee.

"Where should we go?"

"The airport. We have to get to Memphis!"

While on the plane, Langdon explains that taking the letters from SPY and REVEILLE and mixing them together with an extra S—the shape of the serpent—you get ELVIS PRESLEY. And, of course, as they approach the airport, he is sure to point out the Pyramid in the skyline.

Then the next one hundred to two hundred pages involve trips to Graceland, Beale Street (where B. B. King's is located), and the site of the Martin Luther King assassination. Somehow these "three kings" are tied to a secret treasure—namely, the Gift of the Magi—a heretofore hidden stash of gold still guarded by Lisa Marie Presley, who herself, it is revealed is actually a female clone of Elvis.

And when LeBron James turns up, claiming to be the true heir to the fortune, all bets are off, and Robert Langdon is forced to make a big decision.

Sorry, Mr. Brown. I think I'll pass on the book and wait for the movie.

T HE CHURCH IN question was a Dutch Reformed Protestant congregation. I still have no idea what the specific tenets that make this particular sect of Christianity "unique" are, though when asked, I'd often joke that we were taught to believe that Jesus was the son of God, who was subsequently crucified on the cross—although he didn't die right away because a little boy stuck his finger in the stigmata to try and stem the flow of blood. Though his efforts were in vain, he was later rewarded for his attempt to save the Savior by being given first dibs on the first wooden shoes made from the cross.

I don't mean to offend true believers. I only wish to demonstrate that with over 38,000 denominations under the umbrella of Christianity, the more difficult it becomes to recognize any similarities at all between the basic beliefs of some of these offshoot branches of the religion. Much in same way that because there is no standard set of rules for fantasy sports leagues, you will find a few odd leagues that choose to draft a head coach and get credit for each game their team wins. You have some fantasy football leagues that swear by including punters and offensive linemen in the scoring mix. In fantasy baseball, you have some groups that decide to incorporate as many as forty scoring categories, including sacrifice bunts and wild pitches. About the only thing some of these leagues have in common is the sport from which their player pools derive.

On one occasion, our church was visited by a man named John Thomas, who was visiting from India. He wanted to host a kind of cultural exchange program, wherein all of the kids in Sunday school would visit a local Indian church to see how their way of worship differed from ours. And lo, so it came to pass that we were loaded into a bus and transported to the church of John Thomas and his countrymen to experience an authentic Indian church ceremony.

What an experience it was. We were given front row seats but were told we would not actually be using them, since it was customary to stand during the whole ceremony. We listened to the monotone droning of the colorfully robed holy man as he chanted in some unknown dialect. We couldn't see said holy man because of the thick fog of incense that also permeated our nasal passages and threatened to exorcise my breakfast from my stomach with its unsavory scent.

Finally, after what seemed like an eternity, we were escorted into a back room, where John Thomas rejoined us. He informed us that the service was to go on for another two hours, but of course, since we were not used to such a long stint of supplication, we would simply take part in the customary meal before boarding the bus for the trip back home.

My mouth watered at the prospect of food, but that moisture soon moved northward to my eyes in the form of tears when I saw what the customary meal was—dry, flavorless flatbread with a spoonful of overcooked rice and beans.

Eventually, I guess John Thomas realized none of us were actually going to eat any more of the food in front of us—if any of us had even ingested any in the first place—and he told us to quietly make our way to the front door, so as not to disturb the regularly scheduled program, already in progress.

I cannot begin to describe the shock and horror at what I saw as we were marched out of the building. All traces of the incense were gone, and as such, I could clearly see that every single member of the congregation was sitting happily in his or her seat. The leader of the service was reading a story from Genesis. I know this because miraculously, in the time we had been sitting in the stuffy back room, he had perfected the ability to speak fluent English.

Authentic my ass! The whole elaborate ceremony had been nothing but show, put on for our benefit. The last proverbial kick in the groin? That would be the box of Dunkin Donuts being passed around for all the happy churchgoers to share. No "customary" rice and beans for them, huh?

Suffice it to say, this episode is one of the biggest reasons for my present-day agnosticism. But I digress . . .

Looking for some insight into how Jesus chose his disciples, I turned to Jimmy Akin, senior apologist for Catholic Answers. He immediately agreed that the decision to select twelve disciples was by design. "The number 12 is very important in Israel's history. Israel was divided or at least considered or treated as being divided into twelve tribes. That goes back to the book of Genesis where you have the twelve sons of Israel who become the patriarchs of the Twelve Tribes. So by picking twelve core disciples, Jesus was signaling that his church would be the 'new Israel'—the new people of God."

Akin wants to make clear that this doesn't mean that Jesus was setting out to be a conqueror. "Even though Jesus is setting up the church as a new and spiritual Israel, nevertheless that doesn't deprive the Old Israel as having a special place in God's plan. It's not like the church replaces the old Israel which then has no role."

Admittedly, because much of the Bible was written after the fact, we can't know for sure why Jesus selected these specific men. Nevertheless, Akin believes we can make a few logical assumptions as to his reasoning. "Obviously he saw qualities in them that he thought would work well, and that's reflected for example in some of the nicknames he gave them. You have Simon, the son of John, who is given the nickname Peter which means 'rock.' So even though Peter himself can kind of vacillate, nevertheless Jesus saw leadership potential in him, and Peter becomes the *de facto* leader of the apostles before Jesus officially appoints him as their head." Conversely, when it came to James and John, the sons of Zebedee, there was never any question as to their devotion to the cause. Jesus called them the "Sons of Thunder" which not only is a pretty good name for a fantasy football team, but was an accurate description of the pair's enthusiasm and vigorous preaching ability.

Jesus also appreciated the fact that it was a good idea to have diversity in his disciples. Akin explains that there were two members of the group that under normal circumstances would have been at each other's throats. "Matthew was a tax collector and therefore was hated with a passion by most people in Israel because he (worked) for the Romans. At the opposite end of the spectrum you have Simon the Zealot—not the same as Simon Peter. The Zealots were a social movement that played a big role in later years in fomenting the rebellion against Rome . . . but they made peace in the Christian faith."

•   •   •

The Number of the Beast

Twelve isn't the only number with special properties. I asked Jimmy Akin to explain the origins of "666" which appears in Revelations 13:18 and is referred to as the number of the Beast.

"That number has special properties as well. Obviously in English, it has the property of being represented by three sixes in a row, but that would not have been the case in Aramaic or Hebrew or Greek, because for them, the letters of the alphabet doubled as numbers. Even though they would have understood the concept 6-6-6, it wouldn't have looked the same. It wouldn't have been the same character three times. There was one character that stood for six hundred and another that stood for sixty and another that stood for six. So they would have gotten the idea 'we're doing a six thing here,' but it wouldn't have looked quite the same."

666 in Greek: XEC

"Because they didn't have a separate numbering system back then, their letters stood for numbers, and you could just take the numbers in a word and add them up and you'd get a number—and so, for example, you'd find graffiti on walls back then and it would say stuff like 'I love her whose numbers are 545' . . . a little secret admirer's message. People would often combine the letters of words to find a numerical value."

And whose name added up to 666 in Hebrew and Aramaic? Emperor Nero himself, which should come as no surprise, Akin says, since "the Beast is associated with the seven mountains or the seven hills, which sounds like the Seven Hills of Rome. It is clearly a king and it persecutes the apostles and the prophets, and well, that's what Emperor Nero did."

Another interesting fact about the number 666: If you add up all of the numbers on a roulette wheel, you get 666, which may help to explain why so many gamblers have a devil of a time coming out ahead at the casino.

IN CASE YOU were wondering, as I was, why sometimes Jesus is said to have had disciples and other times is said to have had apostles, Akin cleared up that mystery for me. "A disciple is a student, if you want to give a modern word for it. An apostle is an ambassador or a representative. Apostles have authority to conduct business on behalf of the one who sent them. Students don't."

So even though Jesus had a broader pool of disciples than just the core inner circle of twelve, you can use the two terms interchangeably with them because they were both his students as well as his representatives. But make no mistake about it; Jesus was the commissioner of this league.

As Akin puts it, "Disciples could certainly ask questions of their master, but the master is the one who is in the know, so Jesus would not expect to be challenged and have his opinions refined by being challenged the way an earthly boss or manager or coach might . . . Because he's God, so he's kind of really got game."

Counsel and sound judgment are mine; I have insight, I have power. By me kings reign and rulers issue decrees that are just.

—Proverbs 8:14–15

A FTER MANY YEARS of serving as the commissioner of
fantasy sports leagues, I've been able to see what mix of personalities works best in order to keep a league from coming apart
at the seams. Over the years, I've compiled the following list of
twelve personalities every league should have. Compare it to the
owners in your league, the people in your boardroom, or even your
personal circle of friends. Whatever the social situation, if you find
that too many of these archetypes are missing, your group might
be in need of some new blood.

The Loose Cannon: A hothead, like Bobby Knight, Mel Gibson,
or Bill O'Reilly who could snap at the slightest seemingly innocent provocation. A league with too many owners with a fuse as
short as Christian Bale is sure to end up looking something like
Gotham City after the Joker goes on one of his destructive sprees.
We're talking a real powder keg here.

The tiniest little nitpicky thing might send him into a whirlwind tirade. He might go off on a scathing e-mail rampage simply
because you reminded him of an upcoming deadline. Of course,
he's just as likely to lash out at you if you don't remind him. He'll
press everybody's hot buttons, but on the plus side, the loose cannon is extremely passionate and will do whatever it takes to win.
And very often, you'll find that he does.

The Diplomat: A well-respected type who can "reach across the
aisle," whose opinion is taken to heart by all, like a pre-Palin John
McCain, Walter Cronkite, or Pete Rozelle. He always tries to see
everyone's point of view. He is the peacemaker in disputes, and
he enjoys whenever he can mend the fences in long-lingering
conflicts in a "spirit of bipartisanship." Ideally, this guy should be
your league's commissioner. If not, think twice before joining the
league.

The downside to having a league full of Henry Kissinger types
is that real change rarely gets made. Because nobody likes to
upset the applecart, nobody ever steps up to the plate to offer any

criticism for fear of stepping on someone's toes. As a result, rules become stale, and stagnation sets in, resulting in the league's ultimate demise.

Old Reliable: Win or lose, this is a person who always shows up, no matter what the circumstances, ready to give it his maximum effort, like Cal Ripken Jr., Brett Favre, or Morgan Freeman. He's the little engine that could. He never complains. He just keeps chugging along, always getting his lineup in on time and constantly trying to improve his squad—even when sitting in the cellar, 50 points out of first. As a result, he always finishes in the middle of the pack, with occasional forays into a money position.

No maintenance is required here as a league commissioner, and you could do a lot worse than to have a league full of owners who "think they can." Of course, if you do, you may find yourself stuck in a Bill Murray movie, simply replaying the same season over and over and over on an endless loop.

The Ninja: Quick! Name all the owners in your league. He's the one you either can't remember or struggle to think of, but though you always forget this person's name, come the end of the day, without fanfare, he's the one who has contributed the most, like Leandro Barbosa, Stanley Tucci, or Larry Mullen Jr. of U2.

He's always in the playoff race until the final week, and you can't name a single player on his roster. Just like a Luis Gonzalez, David Eckstein, or Octavio Dotel type who always ends up having a huge impact on the playoff race, if I asked you to tell me which Major League team they last played for, you'd struggle to come up with the correct answer.

Fresh Meat: This is his first time around the rodeo, so he needs plenty of guidance and special treatment as he eases into the mix, like Joba Chamberlain, a young Conan O'Brien, or Senator Al Franken. He's the guy who has never played fantasy baseball before. He'll draft four catchers and six middle relievers in the first ten rounds, possibly just because he likes the sound of their names.

He'll finish last this season and the next and the next. But he will win a game or two in a head-to-head league by sheer luck. Will he beat you? And can you take the abuse? A butcher shop's worth of fresh meat can be found looking for leaguemates on Internet message boards. Abandon hope, all ye who enter there.

The Idiot Savant: Why does he make the decisions he makes? Nobody knows. They appear to be foolhardy, yet they all seem to work. Think along the lines of Sheldon Cooper from *Big Bang Theory*, Oakland GM Billy Beane, or Will Ferrell. This owner drafted Shin-Soo Choo and Angel Pagan—amid howls of derisive laughter—and watched them surpass the expected value of their draft positions by a country mile.

This owner traded away Jacoby Ellsbury for the league's eventual home run champion, Jose Bautista, "on a hunch" two days before Ellsbury suffered what essentially was a season-ending injury. This owner should not be winning the league, but he is. Now watch out! He's just offered you a trade that at first glance seems to be lopsided in your favor. Dare you accept?

The Mad Scientist: He's always coming up with unsolicited, crazy new concepts, but every so often actually does come up with a worthy gem, like Doc Brown from *Back to the Future*, Bill Veeck, or Nikola Tesla. He's the type to ask in all sincerity, "Why don't we all draft umpires and get points for ejections?" Sigh.

Yes, he'll come up with thousands of ridiculous rules ideas throughout the course of the season. Then, when the season's over, when the commissioner solicits ideas for rules changes, he won't remember a single one of them. But sometimes, amidst all the madness of Disco Demolition Night, there emerges a flux capacitor, and the league's rules do get a welcome, and perhaps life-saving, addition.

The Cheerleader: Loyal to a fault, especially to his favorite team, his view of the world is always a little skewed, like Phil Rizzuto, Ron Santo, or anyone working for FOX News. Yes, you always know you can get better-than-market value in a trade with this homer; he is the type of owner who covets any player from his favorite team.

There is nothing better than drafting behind a Cubs fan when you want Ryan Braun and he says, "I'll take Kosuke Fukudome." But if everyone in your league remains unwaveringly loyal to one team, drafting only players who share a real-life locker room, then what's the point of going through the motions of playing fantasy?

The XX Factor: He is, well, a "she"—but really could represent any individual who comes from a demographic that is usually not involved in your particular group, be it ESPN's Linda Cohn, SNL's Keenan Thompson, or Mario Cantone guest-hosting on *The View*.

Now, don't laugh, guys. Not only is it always a good idea to get a different perspective on things, but having a female owner might be the single greatest thing you can do for your fantasy league as well. Why?

Before: "Honey, there's another baseball game on? You're not watching that one, too!"

After: "Honey, hurry up and finish the dishes; if Zack Greinke strikes out three hitters tonight, Louise's team moves into third place!"

Think about it!

Captain Loophole: This is the guy who constantly looks for ways around the rules by interpreting them as loosely as possible to fit his preferred way of doing things, like those athletes who try to find an out for their positive drug tests or the way most SEC coaches stretch NCAA recruitment rules to the breaking point.

Any perceived ambiguity in the league rules will be capitalized upon by Captain Loophole. For instance, if the rules stipulate that "the top six teams make the playoffs," he'll argue about what "top" means. Then he'll argue that "make" doesn't necessarily mean "qualify for." He'll drive you nuts! But eventually you'll end up having a league constitution with such clear rules that there will be no wiggle room left for this worm.

The Marriage of Convenience: Two people who share a single vote as equal partners in the decision-making process, they must agree amongst themselves before even getting into the debate at large. Like former Mets co-owners Fred Wilpon and Nelson Doubleday, Cagney & Lacey, or Hall & Oates.

The members of this so-called alliance may own the team together—yet each submits different starting lineups to the commissioner. One accepts your trade offer, and the other one vetoes it. Draft night decisions take forever. One says "to-may-to," the other says "to-mah-to." It's a nightmare, to be sure, but it's one you can use to your advantage. After all, though two heads are often better than one, if you can get these co-owners fighting with each other, that's one less team to worry about.

The Narcissist: It's all about him. Forget what's best for the league as a whole; he's looking out for nobody but himself. He's not necessarily "evil" per se, but you can see how someone might think otherwise. Like Sylar from *Heroes*, Kanye West, or Manny Ramirez. Everyone in the league wants to send this villain on a one-way ticket to oblivion. He'll claim his lineup was a day late because his power went out—and you know he's lying because you're his roommate.

He'll propose the following trade: "You have Hanley Ramirez. I have an autographed photo of Chaka from *Land of the Lost.*" And Mr. Fresh Meat will accept. And the circle of hatred continues. But he'll make an otherwise long season incredibly interesting as you wonder which stunt he'll pull next.

So let it be written. So let it be done.

3

Alone on an Island

I T'S THE SUMMER of 2009. You've got the first pick in your fantasy football draft. You studiously do all of your research, crunching all the relevant numbers, watching highlights and cable replays from hundreds of games, both college and pro. One player continues to stand out in your eyes from the rest of the pack: Chris Johnson of the Tennessee Titans. No doubt about it. That's your number 1.

You're convinced.

It's the summer of 1995. Calvin was mopping the floor of the cafeteria, as he always did after all the customers had gone home for the evening. On most occasions, the task would not take long, and after finishing his "sweep" of the floor and getting final approval from his manager Dave, he'd wring out his mop and empty his bucket, say good night to dishwasher Fernando, clock out, and leave.

This, however, was no ordinary evening. A gun-toting masked intruder entered the deserted lunchroom via the lone door—a door that was supposed to have been locked by Calvin—and rounded up the three men in a bathroom in the back.

When the police finally arrived on the scene, Calvin was found in one of the bathroom stalls bleeding profusely from the head, the apparent result of a blow from the butt end of the gun, delivered by the assailant before he fled, with an entire week's worth of cash in his possession.

A few months later, Calvin had a new title: "Defendant." Yes, Dave believed that this had to have been an inside job, and that Calvin was behind it. Why else would he have left the door unlocked on the one day when Dave took the money out of the safe? As for Calvin's injuries? What better way to try to throw suspicion away from Calvin than to have him get hurt in the robbery?

Dave was convinced. More importantly, the police were convinced.

Back to your 2009 fantasy football draft, as the date gets closer, you're on the phone with your friend who has the number 2 pick. He's talking about how he can't wait to draft Maurice Jones-Drew of the Jacksonville Jaguars. "You know, since you're going to have already taken Adrian Peterson [of the Minnesota Vikings]."

The first pangs of doubt start to set in. Diligently, you go back and look at the numbers again. Although Peterson did lead the NFL in rushing in 2008, only his second season as a professional, with 1,760 yards, Johnson was not too far behind. He was eighth overall in rushing yards with 1,228. Additionally, he also had 43 receptions for 260 yards and a score—more than twice as many catches as Peterson.

Most importantly, in 2008 the Vikings and Titans both had overall offensive schemes that were far more geared to the ground game than the pass. The teams ranked side by side, well down on the list, in total passing attempts for the season. However, in 2009, while not much was expected to change in the Volunteer State, there was one gigantic difference expected on the horizon in the Land of 10,000 Lakes: Brett Favre.

With one of the most prolific quarterbacks in the history of the sport expected to be in the huddle once Week 1 rolled around, there was simply no way that the Vikings would continue to hand the ball off to Adrian Peterson, down after down, series after series, as they had done the year before. In short, Peterson was due for a decline while, at worst, Johnson would repeat his impressive rookie numbers. And if, with a year under his belt, Johnson actually showed any signs of progress, he might well be the top running back in 2009.

Once again satisfied you were not insane, you start pricing Titans jerseys on the Internet.

.   .   .

Three Sides to Every Story

So, you think you know how to interpret football statistics? Let's take a little blind taste test, only we won't be sampling sodas brimming with high-fructose corn syrup. No, for this little experiment, we'll be asking you to decide which of the following two quarterbacks you would have been more excited about having start for your 2010 fantasy football team.

Quarterback A is coming off a season with the lowest touchdown percentage of his career, dropping from 6.9 in 2007 to 5.8 in 2008 to 4.7 in 2009. Last season, he was sacked a whopping 34 times—more abuse that he'd had to endure in any other season. For the second straight year, this quarterback failed to finish higher than eighth in QB Rating, after finishing in the top five the prior two campaigns.

Quarterback B, on the other hand, threw for just shy of 4,500 yards in 2009, which was a career high. He started all sixteen games for his team, throwing only nine interceptions despite throwing the fifth highest number of overall passes in the league. (Percentagewise, that's one of the top thirty-five seasons ever.) His 2009 passer rating was one of the top seventy-five single season performances of all time, tied with Hall of Famer Jim Kelly's 1991 season.

Have you made up your mind yet?

Hey, this is a book and not a televised game show, so I can wait as long as you need. You can even phone as many friends as you like before deciding.

If you selected Quarterback B, as I'm sure most of you would, given the optimism attached with those numbers from his most recent season of play, congratulations. You've just drafted Tony Romo of the Dallas Cowboys.

Now, if you were foolish enough to find the statistics of Quarterback A more appealing, I'm sorry to have to tell you that the signal caller you will be stuck with this fantasy football season is . . . Tony Romo of the Dallas Cowboys.

Of course, because of the season-ending injury Romo suffered in Week 6 (something no fantasy owner could have foreseen) no amount of statistical analysis would have made Romo a winning selection in 2010. Hey, shit happens!

Yes, statistics don't lie, but you can use them quite nicely to tear down a player just as easily as you can build him up. Just remember that the next time a fellow owner tries to use them to convince you that Matt Leinart is better than Peyton Manning.

T HE ONE PIECE of mail nobody enjoys receiving is a letter from your local courthouse obliging you to take part in the time-honored tradition of jury duty. I received my losing lottery ticket in December of 1995; and without a valid excuse to request a postponement, I showed up at 9:00 AM on the date specified, as requested, hoping against hope that once I arrived I would be told that my services were not in fact required.

No such luck. My services were indeed required. Apparently, there was a vitally important civic need for me to sit on an uncomfortable folding chair in a windowless room doing absolutely nothing. After eight hours, I was thanked by the clerk for doing such a good job and allowed to return home. Oh, but I wasn't leaving empty-handed. No, I was getting a lovely parting gift.

"Rod Roddy, tell the man what he's won."

"It's a BRAND . . . NEW . . . admission slip to the courthouse with instructions to report again tomorrow!"

Apparently, there were still a few cases that needed to fill their jury boxes. What fun! The next day, pillow in tow, I returned to the courthouse, but this time I was immediately told to "come on down" or rather, in this instance, up. I was taken to the second floor along with around fifty or so other members of the pool. It was time for the *voir dire* process to begin.

The judge and the attorneys briefly introduced themselves, and then a brief question-and-answer session began. The defense attorney spoke for a bit about the presumption of innocence in our judicial system and then turned to the woman next to me to ask the million-dollar question.

"So, with all that in mind, and since we have yet to hear any testimony or see any evidence in this case . . . if I asked you right now how you would find the defendant, what would you say?"

"I no know. Maybe he do it? How I know? I no know."

The lawyer took a deep breath and tried again. "In this country, you're innocent until proven guilty. Right?"

"Yes, yes. Of course."

"So, you have to decide right now. What is he?"

"How I know? I no know. I no hear what happened. I was no there."

Listening to this exchange, which would have been comical if not for the fact that the circumstances of the debate were in the context of determining the fate of a man's freedom, I couldn't contain myself and let out an exasperated sigh, which of course, was not missed by the attorney.

"You, what would you rule right now?"

I knew I was sealing my fate, but there was no way I could lower myself to be as incredibly simple-minded as my neighbor. "Right now? He's not guilty."

"I accept Mr. Mass as juror number 8."

. . .

History Doesn't Always Repeat

When the 2009 season got under way, Mark Reynolds of the Arizona Diamondbacks was a virtual unknown to most baseball fans. Those who did follow the sport closely enough to know the third baseman's name likely only did so because he had struck out a Major League high 204 times the previous season. However, through the first 64 games of the 2009 season, he had belted 17 home runs to go along with 45 RBIs and was "on pace" to finish the year with 43 homers and 114 RBIs.

I was asked in one of my Internet chats on ESPN.com if I thought Reynolds would actually reach those lofty numbers, and I stated that I indeed thought his successful start to the season was not a fluke. Of course, that was simply "crazy talk" to the overwhelmingly majority of my readers.

The following remark from "Alex from New York" was typical of the feedback I received:

"Honestly I don't want to be rude, but there is no way around it . . . how can you work in this field and say Reynolds will be a top five player from here on out? It could really be the single dumbest thing I have ever heard an 'expert' say. How can you pick Reynolds to maintain or exceed his value the rest of the way when his track record shows otherwise?"

Because of Reynolds's high strikeout rate, and because he'd never had that kind of consistent success before (he had only 45 career home runs entering the 2009 campaign), many people were simply unwilling to accept that I *might* be correct. To them, he simply could not, would not hit those home runs. Not with a goat, not on a boat.

As it turns out, from that point forward, Reynolds socked 27 round-trippers and drove in 57 runs. That gave him 44 HR and 102 RBIs—not too far from the pace he had been on. Perhaps his stats weren't good enough to actually count as a top five performance since his batting average dropped a bit over that time, but it certainly wasn't too far off target.

I don't mention this to toot my own horn (OK, maybe a little bit) but more to show that the "dumbest thing an expert can say" might actually end up being exactly what happens. Sometimes, you really do have to leave your preconceptions at the door.

MARSHALL HENNINGTON IS a trial and jury consultant with a PhD in clinical psychology who has worked on many high-profile cases, including the Jayson Williams trial. He also was a middle linebacker for Cal-Berkeley, before a neck injury ended his football playing days. He admits that the way we select our juries is more show than substance.

"First of all, it's a fallacy that (jurors) can be fair and impartial. We all know that's not reality. They say, well, 'Yes, I can be fair and impartial.' What does that mean? What exactly does that mean? And they give you the rhetoric, 'Well that means blah blah blah. I can listen without forming an opinion.' That's all crap. I know it's crap. The attorneys know it's crap. The judge knows it's crap. But we have to go through our crap routine."

Most lawyers are pretty set in their ways. They've been successful at their jobs by examining the evidence, interviewing prospective witnesses, and arguing their cases to the jury using the techniques that their experience has proven to them to be the most beneficial to their clients achieving favorable verdicts at their trials.

The problem is that every jury is different, and what works on one group of twelve random people may fall on deaf ears with a different set of deliberators. Hennington puts it a bit more bluntly: "The *old guard* is just completely stuck in their ways, and they don't want to change for nothing. They basically look at the court system and say, 'Hey, I've been practicing for forty years . . . I've won millions and millions of dollars . . . I'm not about to change.'"

Jury consultants like Hennington get paid to help lawyers select the jurors they believe will be the most receptive to the arguments that those attorneys plan on making—and they don't just come in cold and do some sort of mind-reading tricks or look for the slightest involuntary movement in a prospective juror's facial expression that will magically reveal their every prejudice. Don't believe everything you see on television shows like *The Mentalist* and *Lie to Me*.

It's not just in the legal system either. We all fall victim to our own individual perceptions of reality. For example, say you lived in St. Louis and were just getting introduced to the sport of base-ball in June of 2010. You watch every single at bat of ten straight Cardinals games, and you've come to one unmistakable conclusion: Albert Pujols must be one of the worst players to ever pick up a bat.

Now, to people who have watched the game for a much longer period of time, it would be heresy to make such a statement. After all, Pujols has won three MVP awards; and for his entire career, through 2010, he has a lifetime batting average of .331, ranking him first among active players and thirtieth in Major League history. He's an absolute lock first-ballot Hall of Famer.

Yet, to Mr. Novice, all he knows of Pujols is the lackluster .194 average he's watched him put up over a ten-game stretch. His reality, based on his personal experience, is not the same as those who have had more time to marvel at the phenomenal skills of the man they call "The Machine."

People have an incredibly hard time shedding themselves of these prejudices, many of which they don't even realize that they have in the first place. As such, when someone makes a prediction of future performance from an athlete that runs counter to the known track record, it's often dismissed as "impossible" by those who simply can't accept that players can indeed surpass their own personal history.

· · ·

When it comes to debating who the greatest running back of all time was, there's plenty of room for discussion. Depending on your definition of greatest, Jim Brown, Walter Payton, Emmitt Smith, Barry Sanders, and O. J. Simpson are all in the mix.

However, when it comes to the television courtroom, there's little doubt that Perry Mason had the best track record of all time.

The defense attorney, portrayed by Raymond Burr from 1957 through 1966 and then again in a series of TV-movies from 1985 until the actor's death in 1993, lost only one case—and even then, the verdict was only the result of his client lying to him about her alibi. (Fear not, by the end of the episode, Mason actually managed to track down the "real killer" though strangely he was not discovered golfing in a foursome with one of the greatest running backs of all time. Go figure.)

But a closer look at the usual line of questioning that led to many of Perry Mason's victories in the court of law doesn't exactly stand the test of time. Here's the way most guilty parties on the show confessed their true guilt. Somehow I don't think the criminal masterminds of today would spill the beans so frequently.

Mason: Isn't it true that YOU were the one who made that phone call?
Witness (*defiantly*): NO!

Mason (*louder*): Isn't it ALSO true that YOU were there at the apartment waiting for her to arrive?

Witness (*more defiantly*): NO!

Mason (*loud enough to drown out both the objections of the prosecutor and the banging gavel of the judge*): Isn't it true that YOU were the one who killed your wife and NOT the defendant?

Witness (*voice cracking*): NO!

Mason (*suddenly somber and full of compassion*): Isn't it true? Isn't it all true?

Witness (*breaking down completely*): Yes. It's true. I killed her.

The crowd murmurs in complete shock at the revelation.

Mason: Your honor, I move that all charges against my client be dismissed.

THE LAWYERS ON Calvin's case were closer to Jackie Mason than Perry Mason. After the defense attorney accepted me as a juror, the prosecutor had one further question for me before he would agree.

"Are you related to Francisco Mas?"

Apparently, he wanted to make sure that I was not related to poor dishwasher Francisco, a recent immigrant from Central America who had left his family behind in the hopes of making enough money to one day bring them to the United States. Apparently, the fact that my last name sounded similar was enough to throw this obvious conclusion into doubt. Just to set the record straight, I am not related to Mr. Mas, nor am I going to find NFL wide receiver Randy Moss at any of my family reunions.

The laughs kept on coming once Francisco finally took the stand to tell us what he remembered from the day of the robbery. English was not the man's first language, and to make things a bit easier on all of us, a translator was provided for him during his testimony. She sat in a metal folding chair just next to the witness box and for the most part faded into the background as I watched Francisco's tear-filled face while he relived the traumatic experience, hoping to figure out how much of the events he truly remembered and how much of his story was the natural "filling in the blanks" that we all do when we don't completely have all of the answers.

Now, during the robbery, the gunman had pulled out some duct tape from a knapsack and made Calvin use it to secure his coworkers. It was clear that ownership of this knapsack was crucial to the prosecution's case. If Calvin had been the one who brought it into the cafeteria, there was no questioning his involvement in the robbery. Although Francisco did not specifically see Calvin in possession of the knapsack that day, he was adamant that "the book bag was already in the bathroom" prior to the gunman entering the back of house. To Francisco, as well as the prosecutor, that meant his friend Calvin was guilty.

The defense attorney, to his credit, understood the importance of this testimony; and as he strode to the podium to begin his cross-examination, you could clearly see the sweat glistening atop his bald head. He slowly retraced Francisco's steps on that day and then asked him to think very carefully before he answered the next question.

"Was it a knapsack you saw, or was it a book bag?"

I'm not quite sure what distinction he was trying to make; but regardless, when hearing how the question was translated, it was clear we were in for a rocky few minutes.

"Era una valisa o una valisa?"

Francisco looked rightly confused, and the attorney pounced at the opening of seeming uncertainty.

"It's a simple question. Knapsack or book bag? Don't you remember?"

"Una valisa," Francisco protested.

The translator, completely oblivious to the content of her translations, responded, "It was a knapsack."

The attorney smugly strode forward, "But before you said it was a book bag. Now, you're saying it was a knapsack. Which was it? Maybe you don't really remember."

And the accusation was translated to Francisco, once again with the repeated use of the word "valisa," and it was clear to anyone who was paying attention that this whole line of questioning, which actually may have had some merit behind it, was turning into a complete waste of time. And yet, the defense attorney was certain after this exchange that he had completely poked a hole in the prosecutor's case, when in fact, all he had truly accomplished was to make the entire jury, myself included, believe he was an idiot.

Is it any wonder that lawyers of this "quality" might benefit from a little assistance from someone like Marshall Hennington? His success, like that of most professional jury consultants, hinges not on gimmicks but rather on lots of hard work. He and his staff study the demographics of the trial venue. They perform community attitude surveys and collect data through multiple focus groups.

Just like many fantasy sports owners, who may participate in several mock drafts—or, at the very least, consult published mock drafts in magazines and on the Internet—before their league holds their real one, Hennington will stage mock trials and go to the courthouse to interview jurors who have decided similar cases to try to understand why they made the decisions they made.

Yet in the end, no matter how much effort is made to select the jurors most likely to emerge from their deliberations with the verdict that the jury consultant has been paid to deliver, it is not an exact science, and ultimately, it all comes down to the twelve jurors. The best that Hennington can hope for is that the people he has helped to select for the job will be willing to set aside any personal experiences and follow only the evidence presented to them during the trial. Of course, that isn't always the case:

"Oftentimes people DON'T do that. They'll say things like, *'Well, in my experience . . .' 'She got bit by the dog. She lost an ear . . . well, she shouldn't have been around that dog in the first place!' 'I was around MY dog. It didn't bite me . . .'* All that kind of shit. You're dealing with that, AJ. All the time!"

"Why does that exist? Because people are a) products of their own environment, b) we are all also the sum total of our past experiences. That's what we are. So what do people do naturally? If they can't decipher in their minds the instructions and abide by them, they have a hard time sticking with that information. The first thing they do is negate that and go off their own experiences and base their opinions off their own experiences and base their decision of the case off their own experiences."

The lawyers in Calvin's case were each quite satisfied with the job they had done, and both sides finally rested. I, however, could not believe the incompetence I had witnessed throughout the proceedings. At one point, the prosecutor actually tried to convince us that Calvin was guilty by introducing his "surprise witness," a desk sergeant who remembered a man entering his precinct office and turning in a wallet he had found. The wallet turned out to belong to Dave.

"This is a smoking gun," he proudly asserted.

The gun in question lost quite a bit of its smokiness when on cross-examination, the policeman could not even be sure of the race of the man who turned in the wallet, let alone positively identify Calvin. Yet, the smug smile on the prosecutor's face made it clear he was absolutely convinced he had struck a fatal blow.

Hennington says this sort of self-deception is typical, and that many lawyers simply don't have a clue as to how best to present their evidence to a jury.

"How do you explain a technical term to a person who only had a fourth-grade education? How is it that you explain cultural beliefs to a rigid individual? How to explain how a conglomerate works when a person hasn't had any work experience? There are so many different areas to tease out with these jurors, so you have to know who your audience is. You have to understand what is going to persuade these audiences. Lawyers are trained to identify what the law is as it pertains to a certain action. They don't have a PhD in understanding how human behavior works."

. . .

Don't Be an Ed

It's standard operating procedure in many fantasy leagues to allow the owners in the league to have some sort of veto power. In other words, even though two owners can fully agree to the terms of a trade, and each be quite satisfied with the result, that doesn't mean the trade is consummated. No, quite often the deal only comes to fruition after being subjected to the deliberations of the rest of the owners in the league, who must come to a consensus over whether or not said exchange of players is "fair."

To me, this is sheer lunacy, as few owners are ever fair and impartial in deciding whether or not to veto a deal. Even if a deal is perfectly balanced and helps out both teams, if it involves a team at the top of the standings, teams in pursuit of the leader will often nix it simply because they don't want that team to get better.

Perhaps paradoxically, there's also a knee-jerk reaction to void any trade made by the worst teams in the league, as the presumption is that these owners "shouldn't be making trades anyway, since they don't really have a chance to win this season." I often wonder why leagues even bother to allow trades at all if they aren't going to let owners make whatever deals they want without substituting their own personal biases into the deliberations. However, at least this is only fantasy football. Lives don't hang in the balance.

That wasn't the case on Calvin's jury. As we entered deliberations, we went around the table to introduce ourselves and to take a straw poll to see how close we were to a verdict right out of the gate.

That's when I met Ed. He was in his midfifties, and as he explained, only recently had obtained his citizenship in the United States, having lived much of his life in Guyana. Clearly he had not yet acquired a firm grasp on the way jury trials are held in this country, as he made the following assertion:

"Obviously, the man is guilty, since he has been accused of the crime. However, if you all feel he is not guilty, then I will vote with you."

No and no! Eleven voices rose up unanimously to correct him on both counts. Not only was Calvin not guilty by the mere fact of his being on trial for the crime, but if Ed truly believed him to be guilty based on the evidence presented, then he should feel free to continue to vote that way.

For those of you shaking your heads and hoping that someone like Ed is not on the jury if for some reason you should find yourself on trial, I ask you to consider how different his view is from those fantasy owners who, when pressed to vote on a pending trade, sum up their view thusly:

"Obviously, the trade is unfair because the owners of the two teams involved are friends. However, if the rest of the league is OK with the deal, then I will vote to let it go through."

AFTER ONE DAY of deliberations, the jury room stood divided, 10-2, in favor of Calvin's innocence, or rather, 9-2 plus Ed. It was very clear from our discussions that eight of those in the not guilty camp didn't care at all about going over the evidence. Many of their minds were already made up as soon as the prosecutor introduced the wallet into evidence. To them, this was proof that "all the testimony" was made up. A few others felt that since they didn't catch the actual gunman, they were railroading Calvin in an attempt to find someone at fault and simply close the case. I was actually on their side, primarily because I didn't think the prosecution had met their burden of proof. However, the two jurors who felt Calvin was guilty had to be convinced otherwise, and "because I don't believe he did it" was not going to be enough to sway the pair—ironically, both school teachers—to change their verdict.

After a night sequestered at the local discount motel, I knew I wanted this case to end before having to endure the so-called amenities again. I also had a pretty good idea that I would have to be the one to do the convincing. In the end, it all came down to the conflicting testimony of Francisco and the statement Calvin had given police at the time of the incident. (Calvin had chosen not to take the stand in his case.)

We all agreed that Dave was still angry at what had occurred (he had resisted being tied up and had been beaten to the point of unconsciousness by the gunman as a result) and wanted to blame someone, and that Calvin was the easiest person to project his rage upon. Besides, with the massive head injuries he endured, his recollection of the events was understandably spotty. His testimony, while full of intense emotion, was irrelevant.

Additionally, nobody thought that Francisco was lying. We all believed that *he* believed everything he testified to, even if the attorneys couldn't figure out that someone *habla-ing español* is not equivalent with that person being an *idiota*.

Realizing that, it occurred to me that *this* was the obstacle I needed to overcome. The two "guilty" jurors were basing their verdict primarily on their gut feeling that Francisco was being honest. If I could convince them that Calvin could possibly not be guilty, without branding the dishwasher a liar, perhaps we could reach that elusive unanimity.

And that's exactly what I did. I said, "Let's presume Calvin was telling the truth when he spoke to the police. If we go over his statement, line by line, and don't find any contradictions with Francisco's testimony, can you then agree that there is reasonable doubt as to his guilt?" It's hard to stand alone on an island. We are each of us influenced by external forces and our own personal experiences which color our view of, in the grammatically specious words of Paul McCartney, this ever-changing world in which we live in.

So you're in the draft room with that number 1 pick.

In the last few days, several owners have already called you with unsolicited trade offers for Adrian Peterson. You've looked at the facts. You've shed your preconceived notions about Peterson *having* to be the top pick. "Chris Johnson," you tell yourself.

You've walked past that newsstand on the corner all week, and each time, that unmistakable purple helmet sitting atop the smiling face of AP on the cover of each and every fantasy magazine breaks down more of your resistance. "Chris Johnson?"

Fearing the laughter and the ridicule if you go with the conclusion that seemingly only you have arrived at, as the clock runs out, you swallow hard and announce, "Adrian Peterson." A collective "duh!" rings out from the room, and your dignity is spared.

Of course, *now* we all know how it actually turned out. Chris Johnson rushed for 2,006 yards and 14 touchdowns to go along with 50 catches for 503 yards and two additional scores. Adrian Peterson was far from a disaster. He finished the 2009 season as the number 2 running back, with 18 touchdowns, but only 1,389 yards. Yet he also had an unexpected 43 receptions for 436 additional yards.

Still, by not being able to get out of your own way, you ended up costing yourself 64 fantasy points, which amounts to four points per game. With many fantasy contests being decided by mere fractions of a point, that difference is certainly more than enough to have turned a possible championship contender into a cellar dweller.

At least you now know your instincts were right all along and perhaps you will learn to trust them the next time a similar situation comes along. As for Calvin, who was found not guilty on all charges, I can only hope I was right.

But I'll never truly know for sure.

4

Sylvia Browne Told Me to Bench A-Rod

WE'VE ALL HAD moments of feeling a bit psychic. Maybe you suddenly start thinking about an old high school friend you haven't spoken to in years and the phone rings. It's her. Or perhaps, for no apparent reason, you suddenly start singing the chorus to an old Thompson Twins song while taking your morning shower. When you get into your car and turn on the radio, amazingly, "Doctor, Doctor" emerges from the speakers. Even the most skeptical among us often marvel at these coincidences when they happen to us and perhaps even start to look for some deeper meaning to their having taken place.

For me, Shea Stadium was the site of a personal experience that bordered on the paranormal. I grew up within walking distance of the stadium, and many a weekend during my teen years was spent in the upper deck, section 3, where I gladly plunked down $4 of my saved-up allowance to buy general admission seats.

On one of these many occasions back in 1983, Darryl Strawberry—the young "can't-miss phenom"—came to the plate. Just as the pitcher went into his windup, I suddenly felt chills running up and down my spine. The usual din of a Major League park faded away to this moment of calm, when it seemed that all 45,000 people in the stands fell silent for just an instant, turning their heads to look all at once. It was almost imperceptible, yet at the same time unmistakable.

In that moment, it wasn't that I *thought* Darryl was about to hit a home run; it wasn't that I *hoped* he would hit one. I *knew* he was about to hit one. Not only that, it was as if everyone else in the park did too, and we all turned to watch. And hit one he did, a towering shot over the right field wall.

A few weeks later, the same thing happened again; this split second of eerie calm, followed by a home run from Darryl. Over the course of the next few seasons, it happened close to twenty times. I didn't even have to be at the park to notice it. It was evident while watching the game on television and over the radio as well—this "moment." Strawberry certainly hit his share of home runs when this didn't happen. But when the moment came, he *always* hit one. And it never happened with anybody else.

Just Darryl.

"I'm generally skeptical of memory," says D. J. Grothe, noted skeptic and president of the James Randi Educational Foundation (JREF), which tries to provide reliable information to the public about the so-called paranormal and supernatural. "Most people can't remember last Wednesday, but we trust people when they say, 'Twenty years ago, this amazing event happened to me, and I'm going to recount it.'"

After I shared my story with Grothe, he didn't doubt my sincerity, but in the words of Roger Clemens, perhaps I simply "misremembered" what actually occurred. As for whether or not there was anything truly going on in terms of some collective consciousness, where everyone in the stands had the same premonition of a home run? The skeptic was, well, skeptical.

"Amazing things do happen all the time. They're easy to remember because they are unique, so if we define something amazing as 'one in a million'. . . we have maybe one million discrete recognizable events in a month, so about once a month a person experiences something amazing. You don't remember all the others that aren't . . . So you don't remember all the other home runs where this didn't happen. You certainly don't remember them with the import that you remember this kind of silence before he swings the bat."

It's like the proverbial fish story. Good old Grandpa Bill may truly have once caught a fifteen-pound bass after a twenty-minute struggle, but by the time you've heard the story for the umpteenth time, the six-hour battle between man and fish that resulted in him reeling in a forty-pound largemouth, along with a thirty-pound catfish that had grabbed onto its dorsal fin, bears little resemblance to the actual events of that boat ride from a decade ago.

· · ·

Paul the Octopus

One of the biggest fish stories to come down the pike in recent memory is that of Paul the Octopus, aka Pulpo Paul. (Yes, technically an octopus is a cephalopod and not a fish, but let's not get into semantics, OK?) Paul garnered worldwide fame during the 2010 World Cup for correctly predicting the winner of eight consecutive soccer matches, including Spain's 1-0 win over the Netherlands in the final. Paul "picked" the winning team for each match by choosing food from one of two boxes, each adorned with the flag of the competing sides.

Of course, while this story was quick to gain legs around the world, as it turns out, Paul was not so perfect a prognosticator after all. Firstly, Paul had made similar predictions for the Euro 2008 soccer tournament two years prior and had actually sided with the losing country twice. Not only that, but according to some reports, the 2010 version of Paul may not even have been the same octopus who went 4 of 6 on those predictions.

Given that the average life span of these creatures is three years, be wary if you do happen to get a "can't-miss tip" from an octopus for the next World Cup, scheduled for 2014 in Brazil—even if he crosses all three of his hearts and swears he's right.

G ROTHE USED TO experience this kind of exaggeration of memory on a routine basis when he was making his trade as a magician, doing corporate shows. "Over a seven- to eight-year period, I'd often perform for the same corporate clients. So, I'd go back to the same client, and people would recount to me a trick they saw me do—that was humanly impossible—something I never did or what they'd describe only had the slightest resemblance to something I actually did, and that really crystallized for me this propensity people have to make things much better in their memory (or sometimes much worse) depending on the situation. In other words, it's not accurate."

People don't do this intentionally. It's simply the way we are wired. These same mental traps that we all experience are what make us all susceptible to the appeals of advertising as well as to those nefarious psychic charlatans. We all partake in what's known as "confirmation bias" where we remember the evidence that supports what we already believe and choose to forget or dismiss the things that go against our presupposed world view.

In my job as a fantasy analyst, I am frequently asked to predict the future. People want me to tell them which quarterback will have the best season or whether or not a certain outfielder is due for a hot streak. What I then do is to look at the statistics and give an educated guess based upon what the percentages say is the most likely outcome.

I consider myself an "antipsychic." I don't claim that my predictions are foolproof, and I am the first to admit I am frequently wrong—primarily because the results of sporting events, especially at the level of a handful of individual at bats, do not always adhere to the laws of probability. But if someone disagrees with my opinion—and that's all it is, an opinion—they will often go on the attack as if I have maliciously wronged them on a personal level.

For instance, in an article I wrote on ESPN.com about relief pitchers, I did some statistical analysis on an obscure, nameless statistic that I called FBA: the batting average of the first batter that a pitcher faced upon being inserted into a game. My hypothesis was that pitchers who had an unusually high FBA in relation to his peers might be in jeopardy of losing his job as a team's closer, the one "go-to guy" in each baseball team's bullpen who a manager counts on in high-pressure, late-game situations.

Managers tend to stick with their closer, come hell or high water, even if they struggle for weeks at a time, until the manager finally loses all confidence in them. I proposed that this statistic might be used as a potential red flag—an indicator of fading confidence. One of the names I included in the mix to be "concerned with" was Jonathon Broxton of the Los Angeles Dodgers.

Although Broxton was very highly regarded, and with good reason, due to his 16 saves and 0.89 ERA at the time (June 26, 2010) the mere fact that I included his name as *possibly* being in danger of losing his job down the line (due to a .333 FBA) sent readership into a feeding frenzy of hate. Again we turn to the message boards for some outrage:

- "Broxton in the danger zone is the dumbest thing I've ever heard."
- "Broxton in trouble? What an idiot! Does he not watch baseball or look at the stats? How does this clown have a job?"
- "Please defend yourself. Are you really this dense? This is exactly why I ignore almost all of your analysis."
- "What you have just written is one of the most insanely idiotic things I have ever read. At no point in your rambling, incoherent article were you even close to anything that could be considered a rational thought. Everyone who stumbled across this article is now dumber for having read it."

Since that last oh-so-clever critic saw nothing wrong with cribbing his insult from the script of *Billy Madison*, allow me to respond in kind: "OK, a simple 'wrong' would've done just fine." And, as it turns out, I wasn't wrong at all.

On August 13, after watching his All-Star pitcher endure nearly two months of a disastrous 9.20 ERA, Joe Torre announced he was replacing Broxton as his closer. While I didn't expect any apologies from the haters, I was still amazed at the extent of denial some people would go to rather than admit that, in this instance, they were mistaken.

"You weren't right on Broxton," wrote one commenter. "You said Broxton would implode because of an incredibly flawed statistic. That's not why he lost his job. You're still an idiot."

Ironically, when it comes to those who *do* claim to be psychic and that they *can* in fact predict the future, people will go out of their way to validate their statements, doing everything in their power to rationalize even the slightest "hit." So-called psychics, Grothe, explains, usually use a tactic called cold reading to try to convince those eager to believe that they are getting communications from beyond the grave.

"Cold reading is where you know nothing about the person. You say either generalized statements, getting more specific based on the reaction of the sitter (the person getting the reading), or you say kind of demographically appropriate generalized statements that you think should apply to anyone fitting the description of the person in front of you."

A psychic like John Edward might stand in front of a large audience and say he's getting a message from someone whose name starts with *M*—"Mark? Michael? Matthew? Does this ring a bell to anyone?" And when someone in the audience responds that their deceased father was Matthew, the psychic will then say, "Yes, I'm getting a father figure." Later on, when the audience member recounts the experience, they will often honestly remember that the psychic told them their father, named Matthew, was there. In fact, all that information actually came from the audience member herself.

"Why is it that deceased loved ones, when they're speaking through the medium, can never say their name," Grothe wonders. "Why is it always a game of twenty questions?"

Some psychics go further into charlatanry and into "hot reading" in which audience members are asked to fill out surveys about who they hope to hear from or are approached by employees of the psychic, who engage them in what the audience member believes is casual conversation. Then the employees relay the information they have gleaned to the psychic, who "miraculously" feeds it back during the show under the guise of "communicating with the other side" and impressing the sitter with his 100 percent accuracy.

•   •   •

I Can Read Your Mind

This is a trick that a mentalist friend of mine (Marc Salem) explained to me many years ago. It works for him whether he's performing here in the United States or all the way overseas in Europe.

Think of a country that begins with the letter *D*.

Got it? Don't forget it.

Now, take the second letter of that country, and think of an animal that begins with that letter—perhaps one you've seen at a local zoo?

Got it? Great!

Now, picture the animal in your mind, as you would see it in real life. Focus on the color of that animal—the real color, nothing crazy like pink and purple stripes. Do you have that picture?

"Why on earth would you be thinking about a gray elephant? There are no gray elephants in Denmark."

While it is not universal—there are always a few wise guys, like myself, who come up with an orange jaguar from Djibouti, which is why Marc was willing to discuss the trick with me in the first place—most people will come up with this answer.

It's not being psychic. It's simply creating the illusion of free will when there isn't really any present. After all, how many countries do you think there are in the entire world that start with the letter *D*? Hundreds? Well, not too many actually—Denmark, Djibouti, Dominica, and the Dominican Republic (and technically, Dhekelia, which is one of two sovereign British military bases in Cyprus—but if you know that, you probably spend way too much time staring at atlases for fun.)

The point is, Denmark is probably the only one that quickly comes to mind, and if you go back, you'll see I encouraged you to already be thinking about that area of the world by my use of the word "Europe." After you pick Denmark, how many animals start with *E*? Earthworm, eagle, eel? Maybe, but by saying "don't forget it"—you may be more prone to think of an elephant due to the old saying "an elephant never forgets." And by saying "at a local zoo," you're less likely to think of an earthworm or eel, aren't you?

If I had wanted you to think of an eagle, I might have said, "Maybe an animal used as the nickname of a professional sports team" to steer you away from elephants. It's no guarantee. It's not psychic—it's just playing the odds.

Oh, and by the way, folks, there are seven elephants in the Copenhagen Zoo—the centerpiece of the Danish nature conservation center. So, don't believe everything a mentalist tells you either.

S O THERE ARE hot readings and there are cold readings—and then there's Sylvia Browne. As D. J. Grothe told me, Sylvia Browne is so brazen and has such "balls to the wall chutzpah" that when she reads she will often just say anything off the top of her head, and if the sitter says, "No that's not right, that has nothing to do with me" Sylvia will say, "Oh yes, it does, honey. Wait until you get home. You'll see."

During one of her numerous appearances on the *Montel Williams Show*, Browne tried to convince a woman who was mourning the loss of her boyfriend that she was in contact with him on the other side, and that he was telling her he had drowned. The woman looked confused and then explained that her boyfriend had been a firefighter who died at the World Trade Center on 9/11. After a long silence, Browne still tried to justify her statement by proposing that he had perhaps drowned as a result of water from one of the hoses trying to put the fire out.

As bad as that made Browne look, nothing quite compares to what she did to the Hornbeck family. On October 6, 2002, eleven-year-old Shawn Hornbeck went out for a bike ride near his Missouri home and vanished. An extensive search by local police, state police, and even the federal authorities failed to uncover any trace of the boy.

As the months went on, his parents, grasping at straws and in need of some answers, paid a visit to good old Montel in February of 2003 to see if Sylvia Browne could help. Browne, for her part, was quite forthcoming with plenty of information. She told them that Shawn had been abducted by a dark-skinned Hispanic man with black dreadlocks. She was very specific in describing his vehicle—an older model blue sedan, with tailfins like the 1959 Chevrolet Impalas.

Oh, and one more thing, she told Shawn's parents that he was dead.

Fortunately for the Hornbecks, Sylvia Browne's psychic abilities leave plenty to be desired. Four years later, miraculously, Shawn was found—alive and well—and was reunited with his family. Of course, his alleged abductor was a white male, who did not wear dreadlocks at the time of Shawn's disappearance, and he drove a rusty white Nissan pickup.

Yet, in spite of all her nationally televised disasters—and there are far more than the two I've outlined in this chapter—the believers still believe, and Browne continues to maintain that she is correct more than 85 percent of the time. She sells out nearly all of her appearances all across the United States and Canada. She also makes quite a living charging a whopping $850 per reading.

I wonder what she thinks about Jonathon Broxton's chances at winning back the closer's job in Los Angeles.

· · ·

Always Bet on Black?

As a former dealer—again, I'm talking about slapping the cards at a casino and nothing to do with slinging dime bags behind the 7-11—I have seen it all.

Most of the people who gamble at the casino understand that the odds are they will lose. After all, that multimillion-dollar hotel/resort you're gambling in didn't build itself. It has been paid for primarily by those wagerers who have no grasp of the simplest tenets of mathematics.

Take roulette, for example. There are many different kinds of bets you can make on each spin of the wheel, but the simplest one is to bet on whether or not the number that will come up will be *red* or *black*.

Now if you go to a casino and ask people making this bet what their chances of winning are, the overwhelming majority will say "fifty-fifty," which is completely untrue. Why? Because on most roulette wheels in the United States, there are two "green" numbers: zero and double zero. If either of these numbers come up, you lose only half your bet, but a loss is still a loss. But essentially, they are indeed correct. The odds of that little ball bouncing around the wheel coming to rest on top of a red number is *exactly the same* as the odds of it finding refuge on a black number, and of all the bets in the casino, this has one of the best chances of paying out. However, it always amused me no end to watch what happened when one of the wheels had a bit of a "run."

For those of you unfamiliar with the inside of a casino, next to the roulette wheel is usually a giant digital display outlining the sequence of numbers that have "won" over the last twenty or so spins on that particular table. What inevitably happens, over the course of an eight-hour shift and hundreds upon hundreds of spins, is that a run of numbers of the same color appears. And that's when the "experts" come running.

After ten straight red numbers, it is not uncommon to see people sprinting across the casino to get a bet down on the next spin. Of course, about half of them are convinced that this is a lucky wheel—and that red is "hot" and will surely continue to hit. The other half are equally convinced that black is "due" since "what are the odds that red will ever come up eleven times in a row?"

Of course, each spin is an independent event, so the odds or the next number being red are still *exactly the same* as it being black. Nothing has changed, except the shorting out of all logic and sense in the gamblers' minds.

O UR BRAINS OFTEN betray us. This is especially true in the world of the casino when, against all logic, we can't seem to wrap our head around the fact that there's no way we should ever expect to win. Each spin of a slot machine is an independent event, with the same miniscule odds of winning the top jackpot, regardless of how many coins have already been pumped into the one-armed bandit. And yet, as D. J. Grothe puts it, for most of us, that simply does not compute:

"When one plays slots, invariably you get this horrible sinking feeling in your gut when you feel like you've 'warmed up' the machine for the next person. You put all your money in, and you didn't win anything. You move to the next one, and someone comes right behind you, sits down, plunks some moolah in, and wins. You feel like that's your money. You just put that money in there; you warmed it up and it's so easy for our noggins to draw a straight line connecting all of those events, but in fact, they're all—every one of them—completely separate."

The same holds true for a fantasy sports owner who gets tired of starting a player who finds himself in the midst of a horrific cold spell. When a veteran player like Peyton Manning throws a total of thirteen interceptions over a five-week period in 2011, with his team going 1-4 and looking lost in the process, and you decide to trade him before his career completely bottoms out, you end up feeling sick to your stomach when he ends up throwing nine touchdowns in four straight victories to end the regular season and secure a playoff spot for the Indianapolis Colts—as if you had any control over his performance. Moreover, to make yourself feel better, you're likely to convince yourself that had you *not* traded him, he never would have done so well.

· · ·

No, It's NOT

If there's one expression that needs to go the way of the dinosaur, and with all due haste—this is the one: "*That's* what I'm talking about!" Seriously, does anyone know who introduced this phrase into the sphere of public consciousness? Because whoever it was has an enormous ass kicking coming their way.

First of all, by this time, not only is the phrase incredibly overused and unoriginal, but it's also extremely annoying. Cheer for your team. I've got no problem with that. "Your guys" just scored a touchdown to beat "my guys"? More power to you. But here's what gets my proverbial goat: in 999 out of 1,000 times this phrase is used, that's *not* what you were talking about—it's the exact opposite.

"Look at these Eagles," you say. "They suck. Kevin Kolb is awful. They never should have traded Donovan McNabb. He can't throw the ball anymore. Andy Reid is a lousy play-caller. He needs to be fired. And what kind of receivers has this team had since T.O. left? Nobody! They all suck. This team sucks. The Eagles suck."

(At this point, Kolb drops back and heaves a 75-yard bomb down the field to Jeremy Maclin for a touchdown and the crowd erupts.)

"*That's* what I'm talking about!"

No, sir, it wasn't.

In fact, it just disproved everything you have been whining and moaning about for the past hour or so. Please go away.

That is the course of action that best describes the gist of *my* discourse thus far.

LET'S TALK FOR a moment about pareidolia. No, not the second baseman for the Boston Red Sox—that's Pedroia. Pareidolia is another one of those mental traps we fall into when our brain tricks us into seeing or hearing something that really isn't there. Ever lie down on the ground and gaze up at a cloudy sky? That's not really a bunny rabbit you see up there—it's just your brain finding a familiar shape in a random pattern.

Pareidolia is one of the main "tools" used by ghost hunters in order to try and convince others—and often themselves—that they've uncovered proof of a haunted house. Most of these television shows involve the use of EVPs or "electronic voice phenomena." A would-be paranormal investigator records his voice as he asks questions in an empty room. Later on, when the tape is played back, sometimes in the midst of all the static of the recording the investigators claim you can hear what seems to be a voice responding to the questions.

What usually happens though, is that, at best, the garbled noise may indeed sound a bit like a voice. But once the investigator declares that the noise is a man saying, "I want you out!" then your brain goes along with the suggestion, and suddenly, that's what you hear. The problem, of course, is that this isn't proof of what the voice is saying. If the investigator had said the voice was saying, "I won the cow!" you'd probably be convinced you were talking to the spirit of a good-at-gambling farmer.

It's not that a certain pair of plumbers patrolling a potentially paranormal phenomenon should automatically be deemed frauds simply because they say that shadow they see is a Civil War soldier. They could honestly be seeing the shadow in that way. However, it's not proof. Yet, to the people who have what they believe to be a supernatural encounter, you cannot convince them otherwise.

Sports fans succumb to the same syndrome.

If you're a lifelong Celtics fan and you grew up hating the Lakers, then to you, Kobe Bryant is public enemy number 1. To you, he is overpaid and overrated. When he hits a three-pointer from half-court to win a game, he's lucky. When he scores 20 consecutive points in the fourth quarter, he's a selfish ball hog. If he turns down a last second shot to pass the ball to an open teammate, you call him out as a coward.

Of course, if Rajon Rondo did the exact same things, he'd have been a sharpshooter, heroic, and an unselfish player who deserves to get paid even more than Boston is shelling out for him now. It's that darn confirmation bias that gets us every time.

I wish that I could claim to be immune to this myself. After all, I know better. And yet I'm still more apt to applaud a Syracuse Orange receiver for a giving it "the old college try" when he misses catching a ball by a few inches, when the same exact play involving a member of the Notre Dame Fighting Irish will result in me snickering and commenting on his lack of effort. In the same way, my brain tells me that all psychics are fake and that there is no such thing as ghosts. And yet . . .

When I was a freshman in college, I lived in what was called an "open double"—a tiny room, big enough for two beds, two closets, and about three feet of empty floor space between the two sides. I shared the room with my "randomly selected by computer" roommate, Jake, who had the charming habit of howling like a wolf for no apparent reason and keeping all of his nail clippings for posterity inside an old prescription bottle on his nightstand. Don't get me wrong—I liked Jake; it's just that he was a bit odd.

Anyway, one of the few perks of living with Jake was the refrigerator he had rented, which allowed us to keep ice cold six-packs of soda in our room, accessible to us at all hours of the day and night. And as freshmen in college, we pulled plenty of all-nighters, during which tons of caffeine was in demand.

We were also, like most college students, extremely lazy—so rather than walk the three doors down the hall to the recycling room to rid ourselves of the empty aluminum cans, we instead started the "Great Wall of Cola" in our room, stacking them along the far wall until they threatened to block the window completely.

Across the hall lived Braun, whom we both were friends with. One day, as we sat in his room talking about this and that to avoid starting our homework, Braun started sharing a story about an experience he and his friends had with a Ouija board. Apparently, as the story went, they made contact with a "demon"; and when they demanded that he show himself, the bookcase on the wall fell to the ground, causing Braun and his friends to flee the scene, screaming in terror. Since the demon was never formally asked to leave, Braun believed it was still following him, playing practical jokes on him so that he wouldn't forget he was lurking.

Braun described two specific things the demon liked to do. One was to mess with clocks by causing the time to jump ahead to where all the numbers matched. For example, he said, picking up his digital clock, it was currently 3:50. "If you left the room for five minutes, you'd look at this clock and it would suddenly read 5:55."

The other thing the demon liked to do was to leave objects in full view of closed doors, so that when you opened it, the first thing you'd see was something that didn't belong there—like say, a blue sponge sitting in the middle of your dining room table, when you knew all the sponges you'd bought for your house were yellow.

It was a very interesting tale, and while I didn't buy a word of it, it was clear to me that Braun believed what he was saying, which made the story all the more riveting. Still, as it was now almost a quarter past four, and we all needed to get started on some work before heading out to the dining hall at five, Jake and I said our good-byes and walked the two steps across the hall to our locked door.

It took no more than five seconds for us to be back in Braun's room. We dragged him quickly across the hall and very slowly reopened the door which we had just slammed shut and showed him what was inside.

There, next to my digital clock which for some unknown reason was telling me it was 4:44 was a single empty can of Mountain Dew, a beverage which had not previously occupied either Jake's refrigerator or the "Great Wall."

To this day, I cannot explain how that can got there, nor how the time on my clock had changed. I tell myself that I don't believe in Braun's demon, and yet . . . let's just say I'm not going to be playing with any Ouija boards anytime soon—or with any Notre Dame alumni in my fantasy lineups for that matter, either.

5

Wall Street and Huston Street: Is There a Magic Formula?

IS THERE A magical catch-all formula that accurately represents success when playing fantasy sports? Daniel Okrent, one of the founders of what is generally credited as the original Rotisserie Baseball League that started the whole craze back in 1980, seemed to think so, and he immortalized it in his league's constitution. Here it is: water, dairy whey, high-fructose corn syrup and/or sugar, nonfat milk, corn syrup solids, cocoa (processed with potassium carbonate), soybean oil (partially hydrogenated), sodium casein-ate (protein source), salt, tricalcium phosphate, dipotassium phosphate, xanthan gum, guar gum, mono- and diglycerides, vanillin (an artificial flavor), soy lecithin, calcium ascorbate (vitamin C), natural flavor, vitamin A, palmitate, niacinamide (vitamin B3), vitamin D3, and riboflavin (vitamin B2).

Of course, put all those ingredients together, and you get Yoo-hoo, the delicious chocolate-flavored beverage that Okrent saw fit to memorialize for all posterity as the only appropriate item for losing owners to use to "soak the head of the League champion with a sticky brown substance before colleagues and friends duly assembled" as per article 20 of the league bylaws.

Technological advances have certainly helped shape the methodology of leagues over the years. In ye olde days, drafts had to be held with all league members in the same room—today, Internet chat rooms make that unnecessary. Once upon a time, commissioners had to perform all the multitude of necessary statistical calculations to tabulate the standings by hand each and every week. Distributing the fruits of that labor required a fax machine, presumably one that the commissioner needed to walk uphill to get to, both ways.

Transactions and roster moves required not only that you make a telephone call, but more often than not, you had to leave a message on an answering machine, just in case your fearless leader deigned to have a life outside of his apartment. Now, free online services make all of those things as easy as a simple mouse click.

The advent of computers has also helped to reinvent the statistical analysis of athlete performance. Sabermetrics, the analysis of baseball through objective evidence, is constantly redefining the formulas for predicting which players are due for declines or surges in their production for the upcoming season. Naturally, in order to come up with a mathematical model that guarantees that you are the one who is on the receiving end of that championship "chocolate rain," a fantasy player has to work a little bit harder than finding the ubiquitous Tay Zonday YouTube video on the Internet.

The question is, however, if that can be done at all. Is there really a magic formula for winning your fantasy league? After all, is it even possible for mathematics to predict something as complex and with so many variables as, say, the performance of a professional baseball player over the next few months?

Back in the 1890s, a professor of applied mechanics and mathematical physics by the name of Vilhelm Bjerknes set out to find a way to compute the future state of the atmosphere, given its current conditions. In layman's terms, he endeavored to become the Al Roker of his time, hoping to figure out what tomorrow's weather was going to be based on the study of high pressure systems and moving fronts and the like.

Bjerknes correctly theorized that once you uncovered the specific probabilistic equations that governed future weather patterns based upon the very observable and measurable present state of the atmosphere, the science of weather forecasting could be performed with incredible accuracy. Unfortunately, Bjerknes was living several generations before the necessary computer technology, and "Super Doppler 4000" storm-tracking software would have made him a household name.

Yet even if the Norwegian scientist had possessed the equipment necessary to join Einar Johannessen on the set of *Dagsrevyen*, standing in front of a green screen and giving out the weekend forecast, one can easily imagine hordes of angry Oslovians calling for Bjerknes's head as soon as he said there was only a 20 percent chance of snow, and three feet of the white stuff ended up falling on Frogner Park.

People, as a whole, simply do not intuitively understand—nor are our brains equipped to understand—probabilities. Just because something has a very small likelihood of happening does not mean that it won't. Conversely, just because we think something is likely to occur, that doesn't mean the odds of it happening are truly all that high.

· · ·

The Unluckiest of All Time

Some people believe that the world conspires against them. They honestly believe that a raincloud follows them wherever they go, and that even when things are going their way for a short time, disappointment is lurking right around the corner. We call these people Cubs fans, and they can trace their run of bad fortune all the way back to a goat.

As the story goes, on October 6, 1945, as the Cubs were enjoying a two-games-to-one lead in the World Series against the Detroit Tigers, the owner of a local tavern, William Sianis, bought two tickets for Game 4. One of the tickets he purchased, however, was for his pet goat, Murphy. Sianis wanted to bring his favorite baseball team some good luck by having Murphy, the mascot of his bar, the Billy Goat Tavern, with him at this important game.

Unfortunately, things did not go off exactly as Sianis had planned. Ticket-takers at the gate refused to let the goat in, citing the stadium's "no animals" policy. Sianis was livid and demanded to speak with Mr. Wrigley, the owner of the team, who told him that while Sianis was welcome to come in, the goat had to remain outside the stadium.

When pressed to give a good reason why, Wrigley reportedly said, "Because the goat stinks." At this point, Sianis was so outraged, he declared that the Cubs would never win again until the goat was allowed inside Wrigley Field and stormed off in a huff.

Well, the Cubs lost that day and the next and the next.

The Tigers won the World Series and the Curse of the Billy Goat was born. The Cubs did manage to win 82 games in 1946, but never were able to top the .500 mark again until they won 82 games in 1963. Although Sianis did publicly rescind the curse in 1969, the year before his death, as of 2010, Cubs fans are still waiting for another trip to the World Series.

I guess Murphy still harbors some resentment.

S UPPOSE I GIVE you the chance to select one of three indistinguishable envelopes. The choice of which one to pick is entirely up to you. Two of the envelopes are empty, but the third one contains a check for—cue Dr. Evil—one million dollars! Next, I'm going to open one of the envelopes you didn't select to reveal that it does *not* contain the prize. Now, here's the million-dollar question—I'm going to offer you the opportunity to switch your envelope for the one remaining unopened envelope. What do you do, hotshot? What do you do?

Ponder that for a bit while I give you another hypothetical situation, this time from the world of fantasy baseball. We're going to hold a little minidraft and select two-man teams from the following four choices. Each day you can only start one of your pair, and unless both are off, you *have to* start one. Now, to be fair, since I've set the ground rules, I'll let you select the two you want first. Who do you select?

- Albert Pujols, a career .331 hitter and a three-time National League MVP.
- Justin Morneau, who hit .345 in 2010 and was American League MVP in 2006.
- Daric Barton, a .260 batter over four years, with 201 Ks in his two full seasons of play.
- Lyle Overbay, who hit .243 in 2010 and has averaged 116 whiffs per 162 games lifetime.

Now, I would question your sanity if you didn't select Pujols and Morneau. In fact, if we had played our little game over the first month of the 2010 season, that dynamic duo would have hit a combined .344, as compared to a very distant and very disappointing .221 from the Barton/Overbay entry.

Yet, here's where it gets interesting—since the rules of our little contest were that you could only start one of your two options each day, if somehow you had started the weaker performer of the pair for the entire month, and I were to have started the better performer from my limited resources, I actually would have outhit your tandem by 50 points, .348 to .298. Further, if we were to have used the statistics from the five "standard" hitting categories—batting average, home runs, RBIs, runs scored, and stolen bases—even though Pujols and Morneau's combined stats would have won four of the five categories (with stolen bases ending in a tie) in our Highlander-esque rules of "there can be only one," guess which side wins three of the five categories? That's right—Barton and Overbay.

Even though it seemingly defies all logic, it was possible that a player who made all the right calls could somehow have managed to steal victory from the jaws of defeat and actually outperform two of the best hitters in the game with a pair of bats not considered worthy to be on a roster in even one of ten fantasy leagues.

Now, is it likely that you'd actually "guess wrong" every single day while I similarly guess right? No, I'm obviously using the benefit of already knowing the results to demonstrate an extreme case here. However, the fact that you would be far better off simply taking *either* Morneau or Pujols and riding them out, day in and day out, is quite apparent after seeing the potential for disaster that does exist. And if this kind of drop-off in performance can occur with superstars, imagine the risks you are taking by attempting the same daily roll of the dice with players of lesser abilities. Surely, every so often you might well strike gold as I did with Barton and Overbay, but the odds are certainly stacked against you.

So, now that I've warned you about the possible pitfalls of not sticking to your guns, let's get back to that initial experiment of the envelopes—have you decided to switch or not, or does it make absolutely no difference? That's the most common answer to this mathematical poser, which is more commonly known as the Monty Hall Scenario. Most people will assume that once one of the envelopes is opened to reveal nothing, that they now have an even fifty-fifty chance at winning the prize. Therefore, they would think, it doesn't matter whether you switch or not. Is that what you guessed? If so, I'm sorry to break the news to you, but that's completely wrong.

When you first picked the envelope, you had a 1-in-3 chance at winning the prize. That means there was a 2-in-3 chance that the check was in an envelope you didn't pick. Because I opened up an envelope that I knew did not contain the check, the initial odds of the exercise do not change. In other words, there is still a 2-in-3 chance that the check is in an envelope you did not pick, and now there is only one envelope that fits that description. Believe it or not, by switching envelopes, you actually double your probability of winning. This may not seem like the right answer, but it is.

I spoke with Dr. Paul Wilmott, an expert in quantitative finance, a field which, in essence, attempts to do for the stock market what sabermetricians attempt to do for fantasy sports—use statistics and probability to predict the future. He let me in on a little secret. When it comes to the world of high finance, you not only can predict the future, but you can also will it into existence.

"One of the hottest things at the moment is called high-frequency trading—which is people buying and selling certain stocks, holding them for a small number of seconds. And what they're doing is they're taking in information from what has happened over the last few minutes; and they're taking news feeds and reading who is blogging, who is tweeting on this particular stock and then they put that through some sort of algorithm, and it says *buy* and then—the average is eleven seconds later, it says *sell* or vice versa, and they hold the position for just seconds and those are just pure statistical things."

To make it as simple as possible, if the computer algorithm that a certain trader has written says to alert them when there are "97 instances of the word *crash* on Twitter" then as soon as that happens, they sell the certain stocks they've determined are most likely to go down in value when that happens.

The problem arises when everybody starts using the same algorithms, and suddenly you have self-fulfilling prophecies. The simple algorithm causes so many traders to sell the same stocks, and then news of *those* sales starts being reported, which influences *more* people to sell those same stocks, which then raises red flags for even more people, and the next thing you know, that predicted huge dip in value suddenly becomes a reality.

The same thing happens in fantasy sports leagues. If everybody in the league uses their own methodology of determining each individual player's value, then you have the opportunity for multiple trades over the course of a season. But if all the owners in the league read the same articles on the Internet, or all buy into the accuracy of the same predictive statistics, such as FIP and BABIP, then they all begin to value players in exactly the same way, making it virtually impossible for any transactions to take place.

• • •

What the Mean Means

Much of the "new math" in baseball revolves around statistics such as FIP and BABIP, which—without boring you with the meaning of these acronyms or the extensive calculations required to determine these values—are used to try identify players who are simply getting lucky (or unlucky) and are due to "revert to the mean."

Proponents of these stats surmise that since the overall league average in these stats tends not to fluctuate from season to season, then it *must follow* that a player who has an extremely high value in one of these categories is due to see a regression—a correction, if you will—back toward the league average. Conversely, a player with an extremely low value in one of these categories is expected to see his personal output similarly rise back toward the league average. This, of course, is complete nonsense. While it is certainly true that some players will have seasons of stellar performance that simply cannot be sustained over the course of their careers—hence the term "career year"—there are just as many players who are simply better than their counterparts, and they not only can, but often do, sustain superior statistics over the course of a decade or more.

Additionally, a player can, in fact, regress to the mean within these sabermetric constructs while simultaneously increasing their value in terms of the statistics that are actually measured in fantasy leagues. It's kind of like what you frequently see in some local newspapers just outside of Atlantic City, where the headline bemoans the fact that "Casinos lost money in April." If you read the story, you actually discover that the casinos, in fact, made millions of dollars in profit, but just not as many millions as they had in the April of the previous year. Success is *always* relative.

I'm not saying these stats can't be useful, but you can't use them in such a simplified way and declare them to be absolutes. Just as you can't expect that after ten consecutive coin tosses coming up heads, the next ten are likely to have more tails than heads as things start to "even out over the long run," you also can't assume that just because a pitcher has "an ERA lower than his FIP" and "a

FIP lower than the league average" that we should automatically expect a regression the following season.

If that were truly the case, Roy Halladay should have been washed up years ago, instead of consistently being one the best pitchers in all of baseball.

WILMOTT'S BIGGEST PROBLEM with the current mathematical attempts to predict the future is that because these attempts actually end up moving the market, people tend to forget the fact that the algorithms themselves don't actually need to work. "Almost never can you say a particular trader is up to some 95 percent confidence level, so therefore, he's a good trader."

What is more likely to happen, Wilmott explains, is that a few lucky calls can end up making a broker's career: "In the first year, you make a little bit of money, and then you use that track record to raise more money. The next year, you do brilliantly; and by the third year, you've gotten too arrogant or the arbitrage opportunities have disappeared and you blow up (lose tons of money), *but* in that second year, you made enough money to retire on, so who cares?"

The same thing happens all the time in fantasy leagues. So what if a fantasy player bases all of his decisions on a flawed understanding of the meaning of certain statistics? He can still end up drafting a good enough team to take home the championship. And while that might not translate to tons of money in most leagues— although it would in Wall Street's exclusive fantasy football league, where the total purse is rumored to be $1 million—what it does do is convince that one lucky owner that he has found the "winning formula."

From that point on, no amount of evidence to the contrary will convince the trophy holder otherwise. And if the rest of the owners in the league buy into that flawed thinking, then they all start using the same formula, and eventually, the viability of the league collapses. In order for any league to last, it needs to have several owners who are willing to think "outside the box" than simply parroting what has worked in the past.

. . .

If Wishes Were Horses

People will sometimes equate investing in the stock market with betting on horse races. In actuality, the two couldn't be any more different.

Horse racing operates under a system of parimutuel betting. What that means is that the payout you receive for betting on a winning horse is determined by the number of bettors who agreed with your assessment of the race. The "favorite" in a horse race is simply the animal who has received the highest value in total wagers, which is then split equally amongst the winners after the track takes out a percentage to ensure they make a profit, regardless of which equine ends up in the winner's circle.

While in the stock market, the value of a stock is actually altered by the number of people who invest in it, at the track a horse's actual chances of winning a race are completely unaffected by the payout. Just because a horse's odds of victory drop from 5 to 1 to 8 to 1 as a result of public opinion, that doesn't mean his chances of winning the race have changed in any way.

Unless the jockey is crooked and intentionally reins in his ride in order to throw the race or, perhaps, does something subconsciously to derail his chances of winning simply because he cannot handle the pressure of, say, suddenly being atop the "favorite to win the Kentucky Derby," a horse is a horse is a horse.

All you do by getting public opinion on your side when it comes to touting the winner of a horse race is a smaller wad of cash coming your way when you are ultimately proven right. So, think about *that* the next time you hear about a "hot tip" from an expert because a true expert would be sure to send you in the *wrong* direction.

D R. WILMOTT SHARED with me an absolutely brilliant demonstration of how hard it is for everyday people to accurately evaluate, in terms of probability, whether or not something that they are currently experiencing is truly miraculous and out of the ordinary or simply something mundane and run of the mill.

Wilmott stands in front of a group of people to whom he is lecturing with a deck of cards, and he asks them to imagine they are in a theater watching someone like Penn & Teller or Derren Brown perform. He shuffles the deck thoroughly and gets a volunteer to count the cards to make sure that they're all truly different—the usual standard magician's routine for introducing this kind of illusion.

He then, again as you'd expect, asks the volunteer to select any card that he wishes, look at it carefully, remember it, and then replace it in the deck and give it a good mixing.

Now, here's where Wilmott takes the parlor trick and transforms it into a mathematics lesson. He reclaims possession of the deck and studies it carefully, finally settling on one particular card, which he removes from the deck and places on the table in front of him, face down. He then asks the audience to answer a question, "What is the probability that I have selected the correct card?"

What always happens when Wilmott asks this question is that nearly everybody in the room will, predictably, settle on 1 out of 52 as the response. After all, there are 52 cards in the deck, and Wilmott has selected one of them. It makes complete intuitive sense—but of course, there's a catch, isn't there? This wasn't an exercise in randomness. Wilmott is performing a magic trick, isn't he?

Once Wilmott reminds them that they are at a magic show, it slowly dawns on most of them that they were hasty in their reply to his probe on probability. After a brief round of forehead slapping, the audience realizes the error of their ways and admits they were wrong. Obviously, the probability that Wilmott has selected the correct card, assuming he is competent at the trick, is in fact 100 percent.

On a semicomical aside, Wilmott shared with me that he once did this exercise at an actuarial convention and had two people insisting that the odds were still 1 in 52, even after he reminded them that they were at a magic show. Once he ascertained the two men were being completely serious, he asked them why they didn't change their minds, as everyone else had, "and they gave me some complicated mathematical argument about Bayesian statistics or something, and everyone else started laughing," Wilmott recounts. "Then someone in the back of the audience says, 'These two guys are from the FSA'—the British equivalent of the SEC, in other words, the regulators of the industry."

In other words, the only people who had trouble taking the human element into account were the ones charged with making sure that the human element didn't corrupt the system. That's quite frightening when you think about it. How can the regulators seek to prevent people from taking advantage of loopholes when they can't seem to even fathom the existence of loopholes in the first place?

But here's the kicker to the whole exercise. Wilmott turns over the card he had selected, and it is *not* the correct card. It's not even close. No, he hasn't botched the trick. He never intended to guess the card right in the first place. After all, if you pay good money to see a professional magician perform, you expect to see a spectacle. No proper magician worth his salt is going to do a trick as dull as "Pick your card. Give me the deck. *Is this your card?* Cue applause."

Quite the contrary—what is more likely to happen is that he gets the card wrong, pretends to be completely flustered, and then actually reveals the identity of the selected card in some overly dramatic way, as in ripping open his shirt and exposing a tattoo of the card on his chest.

(In the case of Penn & Teller, Teller would be submerged in a tank of water, desperately holding his breath because Penn has sworn to not unlock the tank until he finds the correct card. After getting it wrong over and over again, Teller runs out of air and "drowns." The trick finally comes to end as Penn, distraught over his failure and the death of his friend, slowly turns Teller's lifeless body around, and "the correct card" is sitting there for all to see, somehow having transported itself underneath his scuba mask.)

As Wilmott sums up, "The probability isn't 52 to 1. It isn't 100 percent—no actually, the probability is likely to be *zero*. But are people capable of thinking not just a little bit about the human element but *really* thinking about really plausible situations that when looking back are really obvious. If we're dealing with qua-drillions of dollars, in financial markets, you've really got to think of the crazy situations that might occur because in actuality they are not that crazy."

· · ·

One Game Against the Patriots

When it comes to projecting future success in fantasy football, the task is made all the more difficult due to the fact there are far fewer statistics to pull from in order to even make the attempt.

With hitters in baseball, you can find value in singles and doubles, runs scored and runs batted in, stolen bases and home runs. In basketball, free throws and three-pointers are combined with rebounds and steals and mixed with total points scored and turn-overs in order to determine a player's fantasy worth.

For football running backs, there are basically only two numbers that matter—yards gained and touchdowns—and since the NFL plays far and away the shortest schedule of any of the four major American sports, the sample sizes are Lilliputian by comparison. As such, a single freak performance can influence the assessment of a player's value in a big way.

Exhibit A: Ronnie Brown of the Miami Dolphins.

Normally, the rise and fall of an elite fantasy running back is a fairly quick ride, and once the fall takes place, there's usually no returning to the top of the mountain. As a rookie in 2005, Brown rushed for 907 yards and immediately became a top ten running back in many a fantasy draft. He didn't disappoint and broke the 1,000-yard barrier in 2006, but alas, he also broke his hand and missed the last three games of the season.

In 2007, Brown started strong but suffered a season-ending knee injury in Week 7, and his draft stock plummeted as the dreaded "brittle" tag became affixed to his name. When the 2008 season got under way, Brown rushed for only 23 yards in Week 1 and just 25 yards in Week 2. It looked like his fantasy hourglass was out of sand.

That's when Brown had "his game." With the winless Dolphins heavy underdogs against the New England Patriots, Coach Tony Sparano—in his debut season after Miami fired Cam Cameron following a disastrous 1-15 record in 2007—was desperate for a victory. As such, he opted to go with an unorthodox game plan that saw Ronnie Brown taking direct snaps under center and keeping his quarterback on the sidelines.

The bizarre "Wildcat" formation, as it was called, worked again and again versus a New England defense that was completely unprepared for what the Dolphins had planned. Brown not only rushed for four touchdowns in the game, but he also threw a touchdown pass as well. He became an instant celebrity as a result, and teams across the league almost immediately set about incorporating their own version of the successful gimmick formation into their offenses.

Ronnie Brown's final season total of 916 yards rushing and 10 touchdowns once again propelled him back up the running back ladder. He was named to the Pro Bowl after the season, and the next year in fantasy leagues, his average draft position rose by almost 35 picks—and yet, take away that one fluke game, and his stats were nowhere near what they had been just two seasons prior.

Brown ended up playing just nine games in 2009, after again suffered an early season-ending injury, this time to his foot. His 2010 season started off just as unremarkably, as Brown barely managed to crack the top thirty running backs at the halfway point of the season. Yet even then, Brown continued to hold down a roster spot in nearly every ESPN fantasy league. Why? That's an easy question to answer—that one game against the Patriots. People just couldn't bring themselves to either forget it or, barring that, to at least give it its proper label—a once-in-a-lifetime happening, emphasis on *once*.

H ERE'S THE BRIGHT side: because people have so much difficulty in taking a step back from a situation in order to truly evaluate it properly, they can be very easily be manipulated. If you know that a fellow owner is locked into a particular way of assigning value to players, then you can use those same numbers as a weapon.

Go to a BABIP believer and tell them the absolute truth: Miguel Cabrera, who arguably had his best season as a Major Leaguer in 2010 when he posted a .328 batting average, 38 home runs, and 126 RBIs, also had a BABIP of .336, well above the league average of .297. They might just blindly buy in that a regression to the mean is therefore on the horizon for Miggy, and deal him away to you, dirt cheap.

So what if Cabrera's personal career BABIP is .345 which means this was actually a bit of an "unlucky" season for him at the plate. So what if Cabrera had previously posted slightly worse numbers in every major category in 2009 despite having a *higher* BABIP (.348) than he did in 2010? Yes, some people do understand BABIP better than the sheeplike majority, but when it comes to most followers of "whatever the latest trend happens to be," expecting the woolly creatures to delve any deeper than just regurgitating the phrase "batters tend to revert to the mean" is expecting far too much.

A little bit of knowledge can be a dangerous thing.

Ironically though, it turns out that the smarter a person actually is, the *more* susceptible they likely are to being victimized. Dr. Wilmott offers up a "can't miss" way to get the better of someone who thinks they have all the answers by putting them in a situation where it is impossible for anyone to have the right response.

Earlier in this chapter, we discussed the Monty Hall Scenario. Well, imagine you're in a bar and you're tired of hearing Mr. Know It All tooting his own horn. Casually ask him if he's ever heard of the Monty Hall Scenario. If he says yes—and if he *has* heard of it, he'll probably say yes in a very condescending way—act a bit disappointed and reluctantly trudge on with the plan.

Offer to make a wager with him, and make it an offer he can't refuse—give him better-than-even-money odds. Get three plastic cups and tell him that you'll place a quarter under one of the cups while his back is turned. All he has to do is guess the right cup, and he wins the bet.

The quarter is hidden, and he makes his choice. Now, if he happens to choose the cup that the quarter is under, you reveal that one of the other cups is empty and ask him if he now wants to switch his cup. And *he will switch* because he knows the Monty Hall Scenario and knows the odds are in his favor to do so, and he can't help himself but to show you up by proving to you that he knows all of this. Of course, since he originally picked the correct cup, by switching, he loses.

If, however, he selects either of the two cups that does not have the coin hidden underneath, you simply show him that he selected the wrong cup and pocket your winnings. When he protests, you simply explain, "Did you think we were doing the Monty Hall Scenario? I'm sorry. I never said we were going to play by those rules . . . I just asked if you *knew* the Monty Hall Scenario."

Now, don't just sit there waiting for your friends to douse you with a freshly shaken bottle of Yoo-hoo in celebration of your victory. Make like Ronnie Brown against the Patriots, and get out of there as fast as you can—because the probability is that this guy is going to be pissed. It doesn't take an Einstein to surmise that those odds are going to be just about 100 percent.

6

Matt Millen, Bring Me Your Torch

WILLIAM SEWARD BELIEVED in expansion.

The former governor of New York was secretary of state in the time just after the Civil War. He believed that the best way to keep the country safe from any future conflict with foreign empires was to make sure that the United States was the only nation with influence in North America.

As such, he worked hard to prevent Napoleon from installing an emperor of Mexico and kept French troops from gaining a permanent stronghold to our immediate South. He was on the verge of purchasing St. Thomas and St. John from Denmark in an effort to slowly absorb all of the islands of the Caribbean into the American fold before those efforts stalled in Congress. In fact, most of his efforts at expansion—from Iceland and Greenland to the South Pacific—failed miserably. All of them, that is, except the one deal he arranged in the middle of the night in late March of 1867. That's when ongoing clandestine talks with Eduard de Stoeckl, the Russian minister to the United States, finally concluded with a signed treaty agreeing to the sale of what we now know as Alaska to Seward for $7.2 million.

Critics of the deal were quite outspoken, calling the large amount of money spent on a "frozen wilderness" a huge mistake. The purchase became derisively known as Seward's Folly. New

York journalist Horace Greeley wrote that the Alaskan Territory "would be not worth taking as a gift."

Of course, Seward had the last laugh in the 1890s, when the Klondike Gold Rush proved that there was plenty of value to be had in "them there snow-covered hills"—or at least he would have if he hadn't passed away in 1872. To date, though, over $12.5 billion worth of gold has been mined in Alaska, and don't get us started about the multitude of other resources found there like platinum, copper, and of course, oil.

The moral of the story is that you can't judge a deal at the time it is made. What may seem like "folly" at the time handshakes are made may end up being incredibly lopsided in the complete opposite direction a few years down the line. You just never know—and that's precisely the reason why many people enjoy playing fantasy sports. The adrenaline rush of consummating a deal and seeing how it plays out can be incredibly addictive.

Of course, that's not the only reason trading exists in fantasy sports. The days when the majority of players would spend their entire careers with a single franchise have long since passed us by. While there are a few "lifers" left like Derek Jeter and Mariano Rivera of the New York Yankees, there are far more athletes like Matt Stairs. In 2010, at the age of forty-two, Stairs played in 78 games for the San Diego Padres, his twelfth different team since his 1992 debut with the Montreal Expos—a franchise that doesn't even exist anymore, having moved to Washington in 2005. In 2011, Stairs actually signed a contract with those same Washington Nationals, coming full circle in a way, in what will likely end up being his Major League swan song.

· · ·

A Matter of Perspective

Deals that seem preposterously one sided at the time they are made often find the pendulum of public opinion swinging back the other way when the history books finally pass judgment for posterity.

Back in August of 1987, the Detroit Tigers made a trade with the Atlanta Braves for veteran right-handed pitcher Doyle Alexander, who had won 17 games in both 1984 and 1985, in order to help their chances at making the postseason—and help them he did! Alexander was the key to Detroit winning the American League East title that year.

In his eleven starts for the Tigers, the team won all eleven of those games, with Alexander sitting pretty with a 9-0 record and a 1.53 ERA. After Alexander was slated to start Game 1 of the ALCS against the Minnesota Twins, newspapers hailed the deal that had brought him to town for a "nameless minor leaguer." Although Alexander was unable to defeat the Twins in either of his two playoff starts, and the Tigers ultimately lost that series, there wasn't a single person who had a bad thing to say about the trade at the time.

About that minor leaguer who the Atlanta Braves got for Alexander? He went just 2-7 in 1988 as a rookie but then proceeded to become part of one of the most feared rotations in all of baseball, winning the Cy Young Award in 1996 before being converted to a closer and saving 144 games over a three-year stretch from 2002–2004.

Twenty seasons after the Alexander trade, at the age of forty, John Smoltz won his two hundredth career game in a game attended by many thousands of young fans who probably wondered how any team could have ever traded Smoltz away for some "old dude" who won only 194 games in *his* entire career.

P ART OF THE appeal of fantasy sports—especially "keeper leagues"—is that you, as the owner, general manager, and sole decision maker in terms of player personnel of your team, can retain players on your roster for as long as you want. There is seemingly no loyalty in professional sports these days as athletes will often "hold out" and refuse to report to their team until their contract demands are met. No such problems arise in fantasy.

For many owners of "real" teams, though, the bottom line carries more weight than do the league standings. In 1988, shortly after winning the Stanley Cup, fans of the Edmonton Oilers were completely devastated when "The Great One," Wayne Gretzky, was traded, along with Marty McSorley and Mike Krushelnyski, to the Los Angeles Kings.

How much did Edmonton love Wayne Gretzky?

As a nineteen-year-old in 1979, Gretzky scored 51 goals and led the team in points with 137. The next year, forty-three boys born in the province of Alberta were named Wayne by their parents; and from 1980 through 1988, an average of almost thirty-two Waynes per year joined the hockey-mad population of Alberta.

But in professional sports, it's almost always about the dollar, even in Canada; and so, due to owner Peter Pocklington's financial woes, he was forced to trade away the beloved Gretzky for $15 million in cash and first-round draft picks in 1989, 1991, and 1993. The number of new Alberta Waynes dropped to thirteen in the year immediately after the trade and slowly dwindled away until 1998, when only a single son in Alberta was dubbed Wayne. Since then only a handful of newborns sport the moniker each year.

Of course, at least hockey continued to be played in Edmonton. That was not true for the football fans of Baltimore when, just four years earlier, Bob Irsay loaded up a bunch of moving vans in the dead of night and relocated the Colts franchise, which had been a mainstay in the community since 1953, to Indianapolis.

Although he has gotten a bum rap about the move over the years, Irsay's hand was actually forced when the Maryland Senate passed legislation that would have allowed the state to seize the team from Irsay under the powers of eminent domain. Fearing that eventuality, Irsay, in self-defense, simply took his ball and went to play in someone else's backyard. Still, the politics of the situation were little solace to the city of Baltimore, who felt nothing but outrage and betrayal.

It wasn't until 1996 that the NFL finally returned to the Charm City, when Art Modell was welcomed as a hero for bringing the Baltimore Ravens into existence. "This is a new beginning and a new era for us," he proudly hailed as the crowd cheered at a press conference introducing the team's name to the public.

Of course, the irony of the Baltimore fans' glee is that in order for *them* to get a new team, they had to inflict the same heartache and suffering on the city of Cleveland, who saw their beloved Browns pack up and leave town, just as the Colts had done thirteen years earlier. As "Muck Fodell" T-shirt sales skyrocketed, at least the fans in Ohio were mollified to some degree by being awarded an expansion team, who began play in 1999. The team was allowed to keep the Cleveland Browns name, and all the team's historical records were preserved.

•   •   •

Wrangling a Deal

One of the strangest deals in the history of sports took place in the short-lived USFL. When the league started operations, owners bought the rights to franchises; but when it came to where to place them, a long negotiation process ensued, with coin tosses in some cases deciding which millionaire got to put their franchise in what city.

The owner of the Arizona Wranglers had wanted to be in Los Angeles and not in Phoenix, which his team had to "settle" for as their home. As such, Jim Joseph wanted out. Luckily for him, the owner of the Chicago Blitz was renowned heart surgeon Dr. Ted Dietrich, who lived in Phoenix. Dietrich was disappointed with his team's attendance in the Windy City and yearned for a chance to "move back home." So, Dietrich sold the Blitz to a surgeon friend of his, Dr. James Hoffman, and purchased the Wranglers from Joseph. Hoffman and Dietrich then made one of the largest trades of all time, sending all of the coaches and nearly all the players on the Arizona roster to Chicago and vice versa.

The move worked, at least for Dietrich, as the 1984 Arizona Wranglers, who had technically been the 1983 Chicago Blitz, made it all the way to the USFL Championship. Unfortunately, despite fielding a far better squad, the local fans had no loyalty to this imported band of imposters, and attendance actually went down.

As a result, after the season, Dietrich decided to sell the team to William Tatham, owner of yet another franchise, the Oklahoma Outlaws. Tatham then "merged" his two teams and relocated to Phoenix, forming the third completely different incarnation of a football team in three seasons.

And people wonder why the USFL didn't last.

G ENERALLY SPEAKING, THOUGH, teams usually stay in the same location, and it's the players who get shipped from place to place like unwanted holiday fruitcakes. Fantasy owners are, at their core, sports fans and always think that they can do a better job in running their favorite teams than actual general managers and managers ever could. And in the case of Matt Millen, most Lions fans—yes, there are still a few left—probably believe that their five-year-olds could have done a better job.

Millen took over as Detroit's new president and CEO of the Lions in 2001 and immediately took steps to purge the organization of its losing ways. He fired the head coach. He fired the head of player personnel. He even fired Danny Jaroshewich, who was with the Lions for twenty-eight years as the team's equipment manager. Maybe Millen thought the problem was in the way the team tied their shoes?

In his first season in charge, the Lions, who had gone 9-7 in 2000, finished 2-14. The next year, they went 3-13. After just two seasons, Millen had somehow seen enough. He fired his handpicked head coach, Marty Mornhinweg, who had not won a single road game during his brief tenure at the helm. Millen then brought in the former head coach of the San Francisco 49ers, Steve Mariucci, who did somewhat better, going 5-11 and 6-10, before getting Millen's axe after a 4-7 start to the 2005 campaign.

Websites started to spring up on the Internet begging owner-ship to rid themselves of the Matt Millen albatross. "Fire Millen" signs became as commonplace at Lions games as the uninspired cheerleaders. Yet after the team went 1-4 under interim coach Dick Jauron to finish out the 2005 season, Millen still remained in charge. It was Rod Marinelli who Millen turned to next in the hopes of leading the Lions into the annals of history.

Marinelli did just that—by going 10-38 over the next three sea-sons, including the ignominy of the league's first ever 0-16 cam-paign in 2008. In spite of suffering through the winless season in the NFL standings, Lions fans at long last did get to celebrate the somewhat pyrrhic victory of seeing Millen get fired on September 24, 2008, shortly after the first three losses of the season. After the Lions completed their "imperfect season," Millen confessed that had ownership not done the deed, he probably would have fired himself at the end of the year.

It wasn't just that Millen hired losing coaches that made him such a bad football executive. It was his complete failure to improve the team through the draft. After a somewhat successful 2001 draft in which he chose offensive tackle Jeff Backus, cen-ter Dominic Raiola, and defensive tackle Shaun Rogers, Millen selected four wide receivers with his first-round pick over the next six years while glaring weaknesses at several other key positions on the field went unaddressed.

Millen was clearly in over his head and it was equally clear he wasn't long for his job after the trade of Shaun Rogers—one of the few solid draft picks he did make over the years—to Cleveland, just before the 2008 draft. Millen told Peter King of *Sports Illustrated*, "Mark my words: If Shaun Rogers is healthy, he'll be the NFL defensive player of the year." If Millen truly believed that, then why did he trade him away for a cornerback (Leigh Bodden) who ended up being unable to crack Detroit's starting lineup and a third-round draft pick?

· · ·

The Worst Deal of All Time

Perhaps surprisingly, Matt Millen had nothing to do with what is generally considered the "worst trade of all time" in the history of the NFL. That honor goes to then-Minnesota Vikings GM Mike Lynn, who in October of 1989 traded for running back Herschel Walker of the Dallas Cowboys.

It wasn't so much that acquiring Walker was such a bad idea. After all, he was coming off a season in which he rushed for over 1,500 yards, and the 0-5 Dallas Cowboys were more than willing to part with the running back for the right price. But what a price it was!

New Cowboys owner Jerry Jones dealt Walker to Minnesota for five active players and multiple future draft picks, which ended up including three first-round picks, three second-round picks, and a third-round pick over the subsequent four years. Eventually, Dallas parlayed those picks into Hall of Fame running back Emmitt Smith, defensive tackle Russell Maryland, cornerback Kevin Smith, and safety Darren Woodson.

Just four years after the trade, the Cowboys—in large part due to what they received for Herschel Walker—had won two Super

Bowls. The Vikings, on the other hand are, as of 2010, still looking for their next NFC Championship.

After two-plus nondescript seasons with the Vikings in which the team went 21-23 after the trade, Walker left Minnesota for Philadelphia, where he immediately posted the second (and last) 1,000-yard rushing season of his career. The Eagles went 11-5 in 1992 before losing to—you guessed it—the Dallas Cowboys in the NFC Divisional Playoffs.

T RADING IS THE most divisive part of fantasy sports. Certainly collusive deals—such as those in which an owner in last place intentionally deals away his best players to his buddy in second place with a promise of a share of the prize money—are to be shunned, and nobody wants to be part of a league where one owner trades away Albert Pujols for a copy of Ricardo Montalban's autobiography and a box of Boo Berry cereal.

In those cases, rancor is understandable; but sadly, in nearly every case where two owners decide on an agreeable and equitable exchange of talent, every *other owner* in the league looks at the deal from their own biased point of view. Many leagues operate under a policy that all trades are subject to a league-wide vote before they become official, and this is simply begging for internal conflict to tear your league apart. After all, just because you wouldn't make a particular deal, that doesn't mean another owner shouldn't have the right to do so—yet as we all know, some deals are nixed for that reason alone.

I spoke with Yau-Man Chan, who has a degree in physics from MIT, and who currently manages and runs the information systems for administrative, research, and teaching units at UC-Berkeley, and asked him why fantasy sports trades are so hard to consummate. He explained to me that it's because players in fantasy sports leagues are "uncooperative." In other words, there are no "rules" as to what constitutes a "fair" trade versus an "unfair" one.

"In an uncooperative environment, nobody knows what the rules are, and so everybody plays by their own rules," Chan said. "And the idea then is to figure out what the other guy's rules are that he is playing by." In other words, each league is different; and until the group as a whole establishes a collective set of guidelines as to what will and won't be allowed, you have to assume that all players will act in their own selfish best interest.

Yau-Man Chan knows very well what it is like to play a game where people are thrown together in order to try to figure out what the "rules" that determine a winner will be. He is one of the most popular contestants to ever appear on the reality show *Survivor*, a perfect example of "uncooperative game theory" in action.

On *Survivor*, the contestants are initially split into two tribes, which compete against each other in various competitions. The losers of certain designated competitions are then forced to vote out one member of their own tribe, presumably the one who they collectively deem to be the most expendable. However, how the tribe comes to define "most expendable" is entirely up to the group, and that's where human psychology comes to the forefront.

Yau-Man, as his many fans know him, explains, "When you see the (first) episode when we all get thrown on the island, before that, we don't know each other—we're total strangers. We're not even allowed to stare at each other for more than thirty seconds without being yelled at or threatened to be thrown out of the show . . . We have no idea who they are, where they come from—we don't even know their names. So it's basically a guessing game, and the more important thing is that everybody keeps everything very tight to their chests; give up as little information about yourself as you can."

So oftentimes, the best strategy, at least until you get to know who you're playing with, is to simply succumb to the "groupthink" of the tribe. As Yau-Man puts it, playing a game of "I don't care what you guys do—anybody but me" can be very successful.

"So, you say that you'll go along with (the rest of the tribe) as long as you know it's not you (who is being voted out). You can go with that groupthink and by doing that, you then show yourself as a loyal alliance member. But because of the way the game is structured, that they can change the tribes up on you, then that may backfire on you when they do change up the tribes." In fantasy sports, especially in leagues where you are playing online with a bunch of strangers, many league members are fearful to vote to allow a trade to go through when the rest of the league may vote to veto, for fear of being ostracized. Just as in *Survivor*, this fear to step out as an individual becomes less and less likely if you are playing with friends—or over time as you begin to get to know your leaguemates better.

"That is where the social part of the game is," Yau-Man continued, "and you'll notice that the people who win this game are the good social players. You have had winners who are totally incompetent in camping and survival, and have never won a single challenge, but yet, because they are good social players—they talk to these people and make connections and figure out what rules they are playing by—they can now make it to the finals."

By his own admission, Yau-Man did not play a very good social game. In fact, that was his ultimate downfall, as he ended up getting eliminated as a result of a deal that completely backfired on him.

•   •   •

Yau-Man's Words of Wisdom

The best way to make sure you're not making a bad decision is to ask other people what they think about it—and oftentimes, it's not your friends who may simply tell you what you want to hear but rather your fiercest competition that give you the most honest answers. I'll let Yau-Man Chan speak for himself on the merits of peer review:

"We always like our own ideas. If you have an idea about something, you *always* see the evidence in your favor. That's why you have to publish the procedure and let someone else try and duplicate it. If they cannot—I mean, you will *never* be able to see your own mistakes. You publish it for your peers to review it, and then they can say, 'Hey, you fool. It didn't work.' If someone else says, 'Oh yes, we got the same result' then you can move on."

And what about if you're trying to convince someone that a particular trade would benefit the both of you, and they simply won't budge? It's best to not continue beating your head against that wall.

"When someone has in their head a certain way of thinking, trying to persuade them otherwise? That's a tough one. Once they set their minds on a particular trajectory, that's it. Look at me on *Survivor*. . . 'Oh, Yau-Man, he's the feeble old man. He's not a threat to me. He doesn't matter.' They didn't think I was much competition, and even when I started winning the challenges, it didn't dawn on them that maybe I'm *not* the feeble old man, and it took them a while to get there—not until the final five or six that some people started to realize, 'Oh my god, we have to get rid of him.' That was my advantage."

YAU-MAN HAD BEEN part of an alliance throughout much of the season with fellow castaways Earl, Cassandra, and "Dreamz." When there were only six competitors remaining in the competition, it was clear that the quartet, working together, could all but guarantee themselves that they would be the final four. That's when Yau-Man won a competition that awarded him a brand-new truck, and he decided to make Dreamz an offer he couldn't refuse.

Yau-Man told Dreamz he would give him the truck, and in return, if Dreamz won the immunity idol when they reached the final four, Dreamz would give the idol to Yau-Man—thus securing

Yau-Man a spot in the final, where the winner would be decided by a jury vote. Dreamz agreed and accepted the vehicle. After two more eliminations, the alliance of four was all that remained, and Dreamz did in fact end up winning immunity in the final competition. However, when tribal council arrived, Dreamz reneged on the deal and opted to keep immunity for himself.

To make matters worse, though he could have opted to join Yau-Man in voting out Cassandra from the game, which would have at least allowed Yau-Man a chance to compete in a tie-breaker competition with a chance to save himself, he instead completed his betrayal by voting Yau-Man out.

As any outside observer would have easily predicted, the jury—made up of the last nine players voted out of the game—were disgusted with Dreamz's actions, and in the end, Earl won the million-dollar prize unanimously.

However, even today, Yau-Man blames only himself for his ouster. "I failed, in my social skills. Cassandra found out everything about Dreamz. I did not. There was a challenge where we were asked questions about other people on the show—and now, remember the questions are not 'Who do *you* think is the most obnoxious?' 'Who do *you* not want to take home to meet your parents?' They were indirect questions . . . 'Who do you think *everybody* would not want to take home to their parents?' Cassandra got every answer correct. That's how well she was connected with people. That's her social skill."

"So she knew about Dreamz's background. This kid, when he was growing up as a teenager, he went dumpster diving for lunch with his brothers. I did not know that—because I did not connect socially with him. If I had known, I would never have trusted somebody like that because somebody who grew up in that harsh environment could not see very far. They could only consider the immediate future—the immediate action. They don't see that their decisions and their actions have long-term ramifications. That never occurred to him."

"So that's why he had many outs, but he never thought about them. All he could see was the immediate thing—oh, if I honor the promise, I give up my immunity, then I may get booted out, and that's the end of me. Not realizing that, hey, if you don't do that, first of all, you're now doing something that is hated by all the 20 million viewers—not only that, but how about your future, where you have sworn about your kids, and so on—how would that go down?"

In fact, the fallout from Dreamz's decision after the show was clear. The audience at the live finale booed him mercilessly, and whereas other cast members of the show were invited to travel the world and speak on behalf of charitable organizations, Dreamz's name was left off the proverbial bouncer's clipboard. "Now, he has basically ruined his life," Yau-Man laments. "I went to Afghanistan to visit our troops. He was never invited . . . And he never got a chance because everybody thinks he's the type of person who breaks his promises. That's the kind of social part of the game that people don't realize *is* important."

In the end, some deals work and some deals don't. For every time you steal an unknown Kurt Warner in a trade for an aging Dan Marino and you unexpectedly end up getting the league's most valuable player in the process, there's another deal that brings wide receiver Mark Clayton to your roster in exchange for disappointing Deion Branch one day before Clayton blows out a patellar tendon and is lost for the year; and Branch is traded to the New England Patriots and resurrects his season.

That's just the way the ball bounces.

For every Seward's Folly that ends up making our nation millions upon millions of dollars in profit, there's the Guano Islands Act of 1856. This lesser known legacy of William Seward, which he helped push through Congress, allows citizens of our country to take possession of any unclaimed island that contains guano deposits and declare it to be part of the United States.

Let that be the moral of our story. When you make fantasy trades, sometimes you get gold, and sometimes, all you get is a pile of shit that nobody else wanted in the first place. But either way, dare to Dreamz, my friends, dare to Dreamz.

7

Shall I Compare Thee to Tom Brady?

"What's in a name? That which we call a rose
By any other name would smell as sweet."
—William Shakespeare, *Romeo and Juliet*

A S A WRITER for ESPN.com, I'm often asked my opinion on sports, especially once people find out what it is I do for a living. Now, I can wax poetic on many topics: from the 1986 Mets to the Kellen Winslow playoff game to Chris Webber's time-out . . . from the "Miracle on Ice" to Brandi Chastain's celebration. Whatever the topic, I can understand why people would want to ask someone touting themselves as a "fantasy sports analyst" about sports.

But what exactly is a sport anyway? The good folks at *Merriam-Webster* define a sport as "a source of diversion or physical activity engaged in for pleasure." Of course, they also define a sport as "an individual exhibiting a sudden deviation from type beyond the normal limits of individual variation, usually as a result of mutation." While that second definition might explain Dennis Rodman, we'll skip that part of the entry for now. The problem in gaining clarity at the distinction between a game and a sport is compounded by the dictionary definition of "game," which may bring about a strange sense of déjà vu: "an activity engaged in for diversion or amusement."

Why does it matter? Why am I making a federal case about how we choose to define a sport? Well, because there was, in fact, a recent federal court decision that attempted to answer this very question. In March of 2009, members of the women's volleyball team at Quinnipiac University in Connecticut sued the school after it decided to cut their program in a cost-cutting measure. In order to ensure that they kept in compliance with Title IX, the law that requires there to be equity in the number of athletic opportunities for both men and women, Quinnipiac said they would replace volleyball with a much more budget-friendly competitive cheerleading team.

The ruling of the federal courts was that competitive cheerleading was not a sport, as based on the definition of a sport in the language of Title IX: "(A sport) must have coaches, practices, competitions during a defined season, and a governing organization. The activity also must have competition as its primary goal—not merely the support of other athletic teams." While I agree with the decision, I'm not sure this is really the best definition of a sport. After all, under this definition Will Schuster and the kids from *Glee* would be placed on an equal footing with Sue Sylvester and her "Cheerios," and that just seems to be messing with the natural order of things.

Even if an activity does in fact meet the criteria written into the 1972 legislation, that doesn't mean some people wouldn't argue against the inclusion of certain leisure-time activities in the category of "sports." I've found there's one question that always manages to come up in conversation, year after year: "Is golf a sport?" The recent run of Tom Watson in the 2009 British Open, where the fifty-nine-year-old (at the time) legend finished in second place, once again caused that seemingly simple query to rear its ugly head again.

After all, one might argue, if a nearly sixty-year-old man can come within one missed putt of a major golf championship, how much athleticism is truly required to play golf? And if the answer is "apparently not much," then how in the world can it be considered a sport?

To help me answer this question once and for all, I turned to Austin Tichenor and Reed Martin of the Reduced Shakespeare Company (RSC), two-thirds of the three-man comedy troupe that takes long, serious subjects and reduces them to short, sharp comedies. In the past, they've tackled the complete works of William Shakespeare, the totality of American history, the Bible, the "197 greatest films" to be produced by Hollywood, and even "all the great books," distilling each topic down to its essence and getting at what really makes that subject matter unique.

• • •

Speaking of Shakespeare

Jess Winfield was one of the founding members of the RSC and helped craft the original script for *The Complete Works of William Shakespeare (abridged)*, a show which ended up running from 1991–2005 in London's West End. I asked him why he thought Shakespeare was so timeless, and he was happy to expound on the subject.

"We think of jealousy as a green monster because Shakespeare wrote that about *Othello*. We think of lovers on a balcony—we think that is romantic because of *Romeo and Juliet*. So in a way his fame and timelessness are sort of self-perpetuating. He was in the right place at the right time. He was an extraordinary playwright and a great poet, and that lasting influence is something that began then that could have gone away very easily—there was a time in the sixteenth and seventeenth centuries when he had sort of been forgotten, along with all of the other playwrights of his time, and he could have very easily vanished onto the dump heap of history—but he didn't. Part of that is genius and part of that is sheer chance, but it now has a momentum of its own."

We all know the saying "there are no new ideas," and certainly it doesn't take an expert in Elizabethan literature to figure out that *Twilight* is basically *Romeo and Juliet* only with vampires instead of Italians. But how much did Shakespeare actually create and how much did he borrow? Should we really be giving him all the credit he gets?

"I think that early in his career, he traded very heavily in that—he was recycling not only his own works, but also recycling Greek and Roman comedies and entire bits that he lifted straight from Ovid and other ancient sources," Winfield explains. "Early in his career . . . yes (his plays) are all the same—you got your ship-wrecks, you got your identical twins, you got your women disguis-ing themselves as men, and you get sixteen plays out of that: *The Comedy of Two Well-Measured Gentlemen Lost in the Merry Wives of Venice on a Midsummer's Twelfth Night in Winter* as we called it.

"But I think that as he grew as a playwright, the variations on those themes became wider and more varied, and you start get-ting into some of the darker so-called comedies like *Measure for Measure* and *All's Well That Ends Well*—the problem plays as they are called—they are comedies, but they are starting to take on a darker turn, and that's a natural function of artists and writers as they grow older. Life has a way of knocking you around and teaching you the hard stuff to the point that the later comedies are almost indistinguishable from tragedies. And then you get into *Julius Caesar* and *Macbeth*, and by the prime of his career, he is really exploring all of the extremes of human emotion with the great plays, *Othello*, *King Lear*, and *Hamlet*. By the time he is writing those plays, he is really doing something that is totally unique and new in the history of theater."

T HIS TASK OF "reducing" piqued my interest since, in a nutshell, that's what fantasy sports is all about—taking a player's history and what he's done over the course of his career and then defining him as completely as possible in as bite-sized a morsel as you can in order to properly compare him to his peers. So, pitcher Tim Lincecum becomes "a perennial Cy Young favorite, who at the age of twenty-five still unbelievably has plenty of room to improve on his already stellar numbers," and Donovan McNabb becomes "a quarterback without nearly as many weapons as he used to have, and an injury risk who will be lucky to finish out the season in one piece."

So, how does the RSC go about this daunting task? "Our standard line when asked how we reduce something," Martin jests, "is we cut out all the minor characters and unimportant subplots and get right to the sex and the killing." Of course, while that might be a shortcut to whittling down the Bard, it won't work in their latest endeavor, *The Complete World of Sports (abridged)*, a show that attempts to present the entire history of athletic competition "from the earliest cavemen playing 'Neanderthal in the Middle' to your own kid's soccer practice" in about ninety minutes.

Tichenor sees the parallel between their process and that of diligent fantasy owners: "I guess what we kind of do is sort of what (you) do with stats. It seems sort of reductive in a negative sense to take the great romantic sport of baseball and just reduce it to who got a hit, who got an error—to reduce it to math. And yet, analyzing those minute specifics seems to help you get at something about what the meaning of romance of sports is—or the romance of Shakespeare. I guess that's the counterintuitive aspect of the reducing that we do—by getting rid of all the fat, you get to the essence of the thing."

So what is the essence of sports? After setting to the task of reducing it down, Martin came to an epiphany, "We try to, when we sit down, (ask ourselves) how do most people know about or experience this topic? So for sports, sadly, most people don't experience playing it—they experience watching it." With that realization, the structure of their new show became clear; the trio of actors would portray sportscasters who are reporting live from the "Complete Sports Abridge-a-thon"—the hugest sporting event of all time.

But in order to determine what they would actually include in the show and what to leave on the locker room floor, they needed to answer the same question that haunts me like Banquo's ghost. "What is a sport?"

Martin told me they have a whole sketch about Scottish golfers talking in thick silly accents discussing this very topic. "I think what we settled on is that a game is simply 'a competition' whereas a sport requires some sort of physical prowess." But Tichenor added that after further debate, the definition became a little bit more fine-tuned and more ominous. "We ultimately concluded it is not a sport unless people can die. There has to be an element of danger. So hunting, for example, unless the animals can return fire, then hunting is not a sport. But golf *is* a sport, we decided, because people die of boredom watching it."

So, according to the RSC, track is a sport—watch out for wayward javelins—but "Candy Land is just a game, and a great one at that," Martin points out. I wasn't totally satisfied with this definition. After all, by this logic, poker would be considered a game—unless a hemophiliac was playing, since then he'd be risking life-threatening paper cuts by participating. To me, the definition shouldn't hinge on who was taking part in the activity, but in the rules set up to govern them.

After plenty of spirited debate with my friends and colleagues over both many years and many beers, this is what I've managed to come up with: all athletic endeavors fall into one of the following four categories—a race, a game, a sport, or a judged exhibition.

Races pretty much take care of themselves. They are any event, be it a marathon or a sprint—on foot, underwater, behind the wheel of a car, or on horseback—where the winner is determined by the clock. Whoever achieves a goal in the quickest amount of time is declared the victor.

A game is an event where there is a highest possible score a participant can reach. In bowling, no matter how good you are, the best you can get is a 300. In golf, although it's not likely to actually occur, you can never finish a round in fewer than 18 strokes. At Wimbledon, 6-0 is as big a differential as you'll ever see on the scoreboard; hence, tennis is a game.

I come from the video game generation. Once you completed a game, either by beating every level or shooting at "Space Invaders" long enough for the score to roll over, you didn't play it anymore. Been there, done that. Obviously, there's still the head-to-head competition to consider in something like bowling. You wouldn't necessarily give up playing for good after you achieved a 300 game because there's more to the experience than that—but it still doesn't make bowling a sport.

Sports, on the other hand, are athletic competitions in which "perfection" cannot be achieved. There is no true ceiling for a highest possible score in basketball, football, soccer, or hockey, even given the constraints of a running clock.

In baseball, it is true that a pitcher like Mark Buehrle can throw a "perfect game," but even that so-called perfection can be improved upon. Getting 27 outs on 27 pitches might be considered to be even "more perfect" as would the feat of recording 27 strikeouts, which would require a minimum of 81 pitches. Plus, this perfection only refers to an individual position. The offensive lineup of a team playing the sport of baseball can win a perfect game, 1-0, 5-0, or even 500-0. There is no upper limit or ceiling on their performance.

Because of this definition of sport, I would argue for the inclusion of many track and field events, such as the pole vault or the javelin throw, where the "ultimate effort" will never be reached as the boundaries of human achievement continue to evolve over time. However, when it comes to much of what you'd see at the Olympics, my fourth category comes into play.

A judged exhibition is where I classify events such as figure skating and gymnastics, or even an X-Games mogul ski race where outside opinion regarding the level of skill plays a huge part, if not the whole enchilada, of who is declared to be the "best." Can you imagine if the Orlando Magic beat the Miami Heat, not because they scored more points, but because some official watching from half-court thought Dwight Howard's form looked better than Dwyane Wade's when they took their jump shots? Of course not. When there's that much subjectivity involved, it cannot possibly be a sport.

· · ·

The Dumbest Sport Ever Invented

Generally speaking, I like the Harry Potter series of books—even though J. K. Rowling's storyline sometimes stretches the bounds of credulity. I mean seriously, Dolores Umbridge, a woman with no prior experience, positioning herself to take over the highest-ranking office of Hogwarts, all the time warning her detractors to "not tell lies" and overexaggerating the "evil plans" of those currently in power? Not to mention her fondness for tea . . . where does the author come up with this stuff?

But all kidding aside, is there a dumber set of rules that could have been created for the fictional activity called Quidditch, featured prominently throughout the seven volumes of the Potter saga? If you're unfamiliar with the sport—and indeed it is a sport, since there is no "highest possible score" that can be attained—four balls are released into the field of play by the referee at the start of a match.

Operating under "magical bewitchment" several of these balls fly about the field of their own accord. Two, called the "bludgers," try to attack players and throw them off their broomsticks. (Oh, did I fail to mention the whole game is played in midair? Just go with it.) While avoiding the bludgers, the two teams play a hybrid of rugby, basketball, and polo, tossing around a ball called the "quaffle" in an attempt to toss it through one of three "goal hoops" at ten points a pop.

Simultaneous to this action, one player on each team, called the "seeker," is flying around, attempting to spot, and then grab hold of the fourth ball, the nearly invisible "golden snitch" which is flitting about, trying to avoid capture. Only when one of the seekers successfully captures the snitch does the game end, meaning that a Quidditch match could last as little as three seconds or perhaps as long as three months.

Now I would be perfectly willing to get on board with that, if that was all capturing the snitch did—end the game. After all, there would then be actual strategy involved as to whether or not you wanted to catch the snitch and end the game. If your team was ahead in goals, you would. If not, you'd want to play "defense"— simply keeping your opponent from ending the game before your side was able to even the score. However, that isn't all there is. Capturing the snitch earns your team 150 points—the equivalent of 15 goals!

So what's the point of even having any scoring other than the snitch if 999 times out of 1000, if not more, the winning team is simply going to be the side who captures the snitch? It fails every test of logic. It would be the equivalent of if, during baseball games, there were two players in the bullpen playing "pin the tail on the donkey"; and as soon as one of them hit the target exactly, the game would be called immediately and his/her team would be awarded fifteen runs.

Why create a sport where 99 percent of the action is rendered irrelevant by a completely separate competition? That would be like playing two hours worth of "normal" college football only to have the championship decided by placing the ball on the 25-yard line and giving each team one crack apiece at scoring—sheer lunacy!

I tell you, this J. K. Rowling is totally out of touch with reality.

M ARTIN AND TICHENOR were intrigued but not necessarily convinced by my argument. However, as it turns out,
they weren't even able to remain unified in their own position.

Tichenor pointed out that because poker can be played by completely out-of-shape people who simultaneously eat, drink, and
smoke while playing, there's no way it can be a sport. Martin initially agreed with that line of reasoning, but then doubt crept in.
"See, I would think bowling is a sport. You don't have to be in
shape to play, but there's an element of either physical strength,
stamina, or coordination to it. You know, a lot of golfers or baseball players aren't exactly studs."

I agree with Martin that there's a visible difference between a
large 400-pounder with six beers bowling and Tiger Woods swinging a golf club to drive the ball. But we're not talking about athleticism. Jockeys and NASCAR drivers may sit and let their ride do
all of the actual racing, but I wouldn't question the strength and
stamina it takes to do what they do. Similarly, in baseball—which
few people would question is a sport—there is a huge difference in
the athletic prowess of a fleet-of-foot center fielder who can track
down deep fly balls and steal 40 bases each year and an overweight
designated hitter with sad knees, unable to tie his own shoes, who
simply swats 40 home runs a year and little else.

But all of that is irrelevant to this discussion. If a bunch of
physically fit triathletes all sat down to partake in an afternoon
of playing Parcheesi, that wouldn't suddenly transform the board
game into a sport. The definition of "sport" needs to eliminate
consideration of who might choose to step to the plate and take
a swing at it. Which brings me to the one monkey wrench in my
system—boxing.

On the one hand, boxing is a race. After all, the first person to
knock the other out is the winner. Then again, if nobody knocks
the other out, we turn it over to the judges, who decide who
"deserves" to win. That makes it a judged exhibition. Except, that
in the process of judging, they award the winner of each round
10 points, which means there is a maximum score that can be

reached. Even though that scoring is determined by judges, it does seem to want to force boxing into the category of "game."

Now here's where it gets even more confusing. In the Olympics, the judges are there to count punches. The five judges are all armed with a keypad with a color-coded button for each boxer. If they see either boxer land a legal punch they press that fighter's button, and if three judges all press the same button within a second, that boxer gets a point. Under this system, there is technically no upper limit to how many punches a boxer can land, assuming his opponent can endure the onslaught. Therefore, in the Olympics, boxing appears to be a sport.

• • •

Playing Hardball with Softball Rules

Usually, when I explain about sports not having an "upper limit" on how well you can do, an example I often use is that in baseball, a team can hit 1 home run, 2 home runs, even 10 home runs, but it's not like a Major League umpire will ever stop the game and say, "OK, you guys hit 153 home runs, the game is over. Congratulations, you are the champions!"

Having said that, there does exist a bizarre rule in Men's Slow Pitch Softball that actually does place an upper limit of sorts on a team's ability to score. On July 24, 2010, the national teams of the United States and Canada faced off in what they call the "Border Battle." As the teams headed into the bottom of the last inning, Canada led by a score of 30-25.

After scoring two runs, Johnny McGraw hit a two-run homer which cut the United States' deficit to a single run. With no outs, the next two batters singled, and then Scott Kirby blasted the ball over the wall—a three-run home run to win the game for the Americans! U-S-A! U-S-A! U-S-wait a second, why is nobody celebrating?

Apparently, under the rules of this game, teams are only "allowed" to hit 10 home runs each. After reaching that quota, any ball hit over the fence is an automatic out. Kirby was not the hero—he was just the first out.

Scott Brown followed with another blast over the fence that didn't count as anything more than the second out. Ryan Robbins, likely fearful that he might lose the game by hitting the ball too well, ended up grounding out meekly to the pitcher.

I don't get it. And now that I know of this rule, I certainly won't watch it.

M ARTIN SAYS THAT in the end the RSC settled on nine categories of sports, among them being "who can beat up who"—such as boxing, karate, kung fu—the fastest, the strongest, "slipping, sliding, falling"—that would be things like skating, skiing, and rollerblading—sports involving animals, and sports that go in a circle—the most useless of all sports, where you finish where you started. Martin asked me if I agreed that there needed to be a winner and a loser in order for something to be considered either a game or a sport. I think that he hit the nail on the head. While certainly a football or soccer game *can* end in a tie, that's only true when the powers that be put an artificial limit on the length of the contest. In the NFL, the league says there is to be only one overtime period, and if nobody scores, the game ends as a tie. However, once the playoffs arrive, teams play as many overtimes as are necessary until there is a winner.

Similarly in soccer, while regular season contests and friendly exhibitions often end with the score deadlocked, if there *needs to be* a winner, as in the World Cup, the teams do play an overtime period and then, if it's still deadlocked, penalty kicks settle the score. Of course by going to penalty kicks, they've actually decided to determine the champion of their *sport* by having them play a *game*, which is why I'm an advocate of letting teams, like they do in the NHL playoffs, continue to go overtime after overtime until they drop in order to award the trophy.

Without determining a winner or a loser, well then it's just exercise—or in the case of riding a bike, perhaps it is also transportation. You need more than just physical exertion to enter the discussion; otherwise, building a house could be considered a sport; and with all apologies to Ty Pennington, it is not, and he's not a professional athlete. Chad Pennington on the other hand is, whether or not he's handy with a hammer (or if he has any ligaments left in his throwing shoulder).

Now, with all this in mind, let's get to a topic near and dear to my heart: fantasy baseball. Martin happens to be a former minor league umpire who once tossed Andres Galarraga from a Pioneer League game. He plays in two fantasy leagues every year—including a sim league—and he thinks doing so helps to grow his love of real baseball.

"I have all these players that I have a vested interest in. Any game I turn on, I now have a rooting interest in it. Sometimes I have both the pitcher and the hitter, and then what do I do? But I think it's the same with our show, is that sometimes people who may not be at all familiar with William Shakespeare or great literature or whatever the topic is, come and see our show then want to know more—it makes it more interesting when you see the real thing."

Tichenor agrees with Martin's sentiment, even if he has no desire to sit down and catch nine innings himself. "I'm a *Star Trek* nerd and I'll go on and on about *Star Trek*, and Reed will fall asleep, but then Reed will start reciting baseball stats, and then I'll pass out. And my realization was, I like *playing* the game of baseball, but I don't like *watching* the game. The only reason I would care about a baseball game is if Vulcans were playing against Klingons, but I do think our shows analyze the subject matter in a way that makes people interested."

So while we consider Tichenor's concept of fantasy baseball as one incorporating Seven of Nine turning a 6-4-3, we still have one last question we need to address. Is "fantasy sports" itself a sport? The answer comes down to whether or not there is a highest-possible score a fantasy owner can reach, and I'd say that there is.

Certainly if a fantasy basketball owner drafts LeBron James, James himself can score 20, 40, 60, or 100 points in a given basketball game. Over the course of the season, James has no artificial ceiling placed on his scoring. But for the fantasy owner who drafts him, all he can do is either insert him into the starting lineup or not. He gets whatever James gives him, and he has no control over that final number.

Yes, an owner can trade players and try to maximize returns, or he can attempt to sub players in and out on a daily basis hoping to somehow catch all the hot streaks and avoid all of the cold streaks in a player's season; but in the end, the ceiling on your score is determined by whatever the players do on the court. You can't do better than get "the highest possible point total" that your decisions as a fantasy owner will permit.

Therefore, fantasy sports in my view is a misnomer; it's really a fantasy game. But it's a great game—even better than Candy Land.

Exeunt.

8

Looking for Kevin Love
in All the Wrong Places

T HEY SAY THAT patience is a virtue. They also say that he who hesitates is lost. But then they recommend that you look before you leap, but not to look a gift horse in the mouth, unless of course you got the present in question from Nia Vardalos, since we are to be wary of Greeks bearing gifts. Personally, I think it's probably best if we think for ourselves and get "they" the number of a good psychotherapist.

Truth be told, when it comes to fantasy sports, we're frequently driven to the brink of insanity by players who on the surface appear to have all the perfect qualities to achieve success and yet frustrate the hell out of their owners by going through extreme ebbs and flows in performance.

Kevin Love's rookie season was a prime example of this whirlwind roller-coaster ride on which some athletes will take their fantasy owners. In 2007, Love had a phenomenal season as a freshman at UCLA. He scored 17.5 points per game and averaged over ten rebounds per contest en route to a Final Four appearance for the Bruins. Love was named as a first-team All-American, as well as the Pac-10 Player of the Year.

The NBA was quite smitten with Love, and he knew it. As such, he decided to forego his final three seasons of college eligibility and enter the 2008 NBA Draft, where he was selected with the fifth overall pick by the Memphis Grizzlies, who then opted to "share the Love" by turning around and trading his highly coveted rights in a multiplayer deal to the Minnesota Timberwolves.

Not all fantasy owners were convinced at first, but after watching Love score almost 12 points per game over his first five appearances as a rookie, he was a popular waiver wire selection in many fantasy hoops leagues. Unfortunately, over Love's next nine games, his scoring output dropped to under six points per game, and suddenly Love no longer seemed like such a many-splendored thing. Back to the waiver wire with him!

Cue the music of the Ohio Players on your iPod as we take you through the rest of Love's rookie season. The next seven games: a 12.1 points per game (PPG) average. Sign him! The following eight: 2.8 PPG. Cut him! And on it went, with his performance constantly turning on a dime. December 29: 17 points, December 30: a goose egg, January 2: 19 points, January 6: 6 points, January 7: 16 points, January 10: 5 points.

Every time you thought Love might be turning a corner, he'd seemingly suffer a setback. He scored a season-high 24 points on February 25 against Utah, only to be held to a single bucket in the game against Portland two nights later. The 23 points he scored on March 31 against the Dallas Mavericks turned out to be an early April Fools' gag as he tallied only 2 points in his next game against Utah.

C. S. Lewis once wrote, "Why love if losing hurts so much?" In this case, why Love indeed? He was the cause of many fantasy basketball teams dying a slow death, as more often than not, though his fantasy owners' hearts were in the right place, their timing just wasn't right.

. . .

Faulty First Impressions

Strike One: On April 4, 1994, a previously unknown outfielder for the Chicago Cubs burst into the public consciousness by belting three Opening Day home runs off New York Mets' ace Dwight Gooden. Tuffy Rhodes was suddenly an incredibly hot commodity in fantasy baseball leagues across the country.

He finished up the month of April with 6 home runs and a .313 batting average, then proceeded to stink up the joint for the rest of the season, hitting a sad .201 from May 1 on, with only 2 more round-trippers to his name.

Strike Two: In Week 1 of the 2005 NFL season, undrafted wide receiver Frisman Jackson of the Cleveland Browns had a masterful day against the Cincinnati Bengals, catching eight passes for 128 yards and a touchdown. Guess who was first pick off the waiver wire before Week 2 games got under way?

Sadly for Jackson, a rookie by the name of Braylon Edwards caught three balls for 107 yards and a score in Week 2 and went on to become a star. Jackson caught only a handful of passes the rest of the season and never again made a professional roster.

Strike Three: Young Red Sox pitcher Devern Hansack got a late-season call-up in 2006, and on the final day of the regular season, in only his second big league start, he threw a rain-shortened no-hitter. The following season, when he got called up from the minor leagues in May due to injuries to multiple Boston pitchers, more than a few fantasy owners remembered the "no-no" and took a shot in the dark.

Hansack lasted only four innings in a May 19, 2007, start and the Red Sox lost 14-0. Apart from one relief appearance that September, and a cup of coffee in 2008, he never again pitched in the majors.

You're out!

S TEVE WARD KNOWS a lot about what makes relationships
work. You may know the professional matchmaker from his
VH1 program *Tough Love*, where he runs a bunch of women who
have been unlucky in love through a "dating boot camp" to try to
get them to learn the mistakes they are making—and repeating
over and over—in their pursuit of happiness.

Ward is also a big sports fan, particularly of his hometown
Philadelphia teams, and he says one of the most common things
that people forget is that they are, in fact, allowed to make their
own decisions and not become slaves to the opinions of others.

"I think the one mistake that a lot of people make—when it
comes to either drafting players in a fantasy league or even making
the decision to enter a relationship with somebody is that they rely
on other people's assessments, the so-called experts and profes-
sionals. And hey, look, I am one of those (experts) so I'll be the
first one to tell you that it's just an opinion that we're offering. It's
just our educated guess, and the fact of the matter is that a lot of
people end up being busts."

Ward says that when you're trying to decide if that hot prospect
is going to have a successful professional career, you look at the
pedigree. What college did they go to? What conference did they
play in? What kind of coaches did they have? Were they drafted
into an organization with the same type of system in which they
enjoyed success in college?

The same thing holds true for that hot girl sitting across from
you during a speed-dating session. You have a very limited amount
of time to make an assessment as to whether or not you want to
spend more time with this person, and you need to use it wisely.

"So you meet someone at a speed date, and you say to yourself,
all right this is someone who I think is really attractive, it seems like
there is a little bit of chemistry between the two of us, and I really
like what they're saying . . . *but* I also learn that they live in a different part of town, and that they didn't finish college, and I know
that my family probably wouldn't appreciate this person or I'm

going to have to deal with 'this' because of 'that' or the commute's going to be a pain in the butt, or *yada yada yada*. You make your decision based on external factors that really do affect your choice to, in many respects, 'draft' that person for your relationship."

So just as you may draft a less-talented player onto your fantasy team because he is in a situation where is more likely to succeed than perhaps someone who has more ability, but is in an organization—even one with a better chance at winning games—where is likely to be underutilized, so too does it make sense to choose to pursue a relationship with greater odds of succeeding and with fewer built-in obstacles. As Ward puts it, "You don't decide to go into a relationship with someone just because they come from a really great family."

I used to belong to an improvisational comedy troupe in New York City, acting off-Broadway without a script, making things up as we went along. People would often come up to me after a successful show and marvel over our ability to pull it off. Although, when done well, improv is certainly harder than it looks; the fact is that unless you woke up this morning with a script on your nightstand, telling you what to do and what to say over the next twenty-four hours, then you, too, are an improviser of sorts.

Life has no script, and neither does love. That's something that clearly seemed to be lost on some of Ward's wards who had constructed elaborate point systems to judge the quality of their dates or long lists of qualifications with such high standards that no actual, real-life man could ever meet their irrational expectations.

Ward couldn't agree more that in order to succeed at anything, be it dating or fantasy sports—whatever it is—you sometimes need to be able to think on your feet and be flexible. "A lot of times, people's drafts get blown up because the people in front of them make decisions that totally impact their plan. But that's the thing—the best coaches that are out there in any sport are the ones who are able to adapt and improvise and change their game plan. The coach who can go into halftime and make those adjustments and come out and change the momentum of the game is ultimately the best coach that there is."

. . .

Always Say "Yes"

While it may sound like the plot of a really bad Jim Carrey movie, the fact is that "always say yes" is one of the two "rules of improv." We'll discuss the second rule later, but rest assured it has nothing to do with *Ace Ventura*, where the only thing you could possibly glean from the hilarity that ensues from that bit of cinematic fluff is "when in doubt, make ass noises."

Imagine you're going on stage in front of an audience—a paying audience with bloodlust in their eyes, ready to charge the stage with pitchforks if you truly suck—with no script to fall back on. It's just you and one other actor. What could you possibly say to start the scene?

If you're like most people, you'll say nothing, afraid that anything you say will be the wrong thing. Unfortunately, self-censorship is the death knell for improv performers. And so, the two actors stand there staring at each other, each one afraid to make the first move, for fear that it "won't be funny."

That's where your first rule of improv comes into play: always say yes to any offer that your fellow performer makes. What's an offer? It can be anything: a line of dialogue, picking up a prop, even an involuntary physical action, such as shivering, could be inspiration for you to say, "Let me get you a coat, you look cold."

What you don't want to do is to negate the reality of the initial offer your partner makes. That's a recipe for certain disaster. For example, if your scene partner sets up an elaborate pantomime of getting into a car, and then calls out to you saying, "Are you coming down? We don't want to be late for Susie's graduation!" you don't want to say, "Shut up, Grandma. You know Susie's dead.

Now come and get inside off this ledge before the neighbors call the cops!" Sure, it may get a cheap laugh from the audience, but it has not only effectively derailed the scene, it has also probably guaranteed this performer will never want to work with you again. Improv acting demands that you play as a team.

Now, of course, in fantasy sports you don't want to automatically say "yes" when someone offers to trade you the likes of Thabo Sefolosha for LeBron James, but there are "degrees of yes." It's far better to respond by saying, "You know, I *could* use a little help with my depth at guard. Maybe we can arrange a deal that's a little less one sided" than to say something nasty that permanently eliminates one potential trade partner from the equation.

ALTHOUGH THERE ARE few things that have as much impact on a person's emotions as dating clearly does, Ward feels it is essential that when dating, you attempt to remain on as even a keel as possible, lest you lose sight of the ultimate goal—a fulfilling, long-lasting relationship. He suggests that's a lesson fantasy owners shouldn't lose sight of either.

"There's a certain element of control in (fantasy sports). If things are going bad, you can just walk away. You know that you're not dealing with—most of the time—with elements that are actually within your control, so that by having that stripped away from you, in that one sense, you're almost given *more* control because you're the only one who has emotions invested in it."

However, just because you *can* walk away, that doesn't mean you should. "It's like when you're watching Brian Westbrook, for example, who is trying to run out the clock in his game and doesn't want to give the other team an opportunity to get the ball back. And he starts running around and kneels down on the 1-yard line, rather than crossing the goal and scoring a touchdown. As a fantasy owner, you can't say, 'I'm going to cut him this week' or 'I'm not going to start him because he didn't go for the touchdown. He didn't get me those points that I wanted.'"

But while you don't want to overreact to one particular incident and end a relationship before you know for sure that there's no future in it for you, there is definitely a tipping point that is reached, where enough is definitely enough and it is time to move on. That's when, as Marcellus Wallace from *Pulp Fiction* warns prize fighter Butch, you have to make sure you ignore that sting of pride.

Case in point, the Oakland Raiders selected quarterback JaMarcus Russell with the number one overall pick in the 2007 NFL Draft. After Russell held out for all of training camp, he finally signed with the team for six years and $68 million, almost half of which was guaranteed.

He played very sparingly in his rookie season but was named the team's starter for 2008, and well, there's no way to sugarcoat the results: Russell stunk up the joint, winning five games while losing ten, and only topping 250 yards passing a single time, while failing to top 150 yards on ten occasions.

Nevertheless, the Raiders had invested an awful lot of money on Russell, so when 2009 came around, guess who got the call as the Week 1 starter? After a 2-7 start to the season, and only two games during which he managed to surpass 200 yards through the air, Russell was finally, mercifully, benched. His final stats for the season had him ranked dead last among qualified quarterbacks in QB Rating, the league's standard measure for determining the value of a player at his position.

Finally, after reports of Russell reporting to training camp in 2010 overweight, and with the prospect of paying him $9 million if he made the roster, the Raiders finally admitted what everyone else already knew: Russell was not an NFL quarterback. They released him in May. No other team bothered to make him an offer, even at the league's minimum salary.

"Pride is what it boils down to," Ward says. "The ancient Greeks used to have a word for it. They called it *hubris*—excessive pride to the point of costliness to others. It used to be a capital offense. You could be executed in ancient Greece if you were found guilty of this. Can you imagine if Al Davis was alive in Ancient Greece? He'd be dead!"

Whether you're talking about fantasy football or real relationships, all you're really asking for is consistency. You don't want someone who is going to give you one terrific "night you'll never forget" followed by ten miserable "when will this be over" outings. You want someone who you can rely on, week in and week out.

"You don't need someone to put up the most points every single week, but to put up a certain amount of points and you know you can depend on them—you can count on them—that's the point of getting married. That's the point of being committed to long-term relationships, so you can really have the security with that person. You don't want to speculate in fantasy any more than you want to speculate in your relationships."

• • •

Rule Number 2: Make Your Partner Look Good

There's a reason that public speaking always ranks so high on surveys of people's fears. It's scary. Putting yourself out there in front of a crowd with the spotlight shining solely on you can be very intimidating, and if you're attempting to add a bit of humor into the mix and your opening salvo goes over like a lead balloon, it's likely to become a disaster of *Hindenburg* proportions—and that's with a scripted speech that you've probably rehearsed several times over.

Imagine now going on the stage without a net—no script—just you and your scene partner. It's only human to be a little nervous and perhaps a bit self-focused. "What am I going to say next?"

"Are they going to laugh at me, for the right reasons?" "Are they going to hate me?" Unfortunately, while all these thoughts are running through your head, you just missed the fact that your partner established the scene by pantomiming building a campfire and asked you if you wanted marshmallows. Now he's looking at you, and sadly, you have nothing to add to the scene but a blank stare. Hello, disaster.

That's why the second rule of improv is what it is. By not focusing on yourself, but on your partner, you're sure to stay attuned to what is actually being done and said on stage, as opposed to lost in thought about the infinite possibilities of what might come. But the rule is more than just "look at your partner"—it's "make your partner look good." That also means not stealing the spotlight at the expense of the narrative or throwing them under the bus for the sake of an easy laugh.

Applying this rule to the world of fantasy sports will help you in the long run when it comes to trading. Why? Because it's far more likely someone will agree to a swap when you craft a deal that makes *their* roster more formidable while simultaneously improving your own squad, rather than hoping to pull off some major swindle.

Besides, even if you do succeed at pulling the wool over your "victim's" eyes, such tactics are likely to have the rest of your league up in arms over your chicanery and you may never be able to get anyone to trade with you ever again. As our old friends "they" say, don't throw out the baby with the bathwater, cut off your nose to spite your own face, or go crying over spilt milk, especially when you can have your cake and eat it too.

N O MATTER HOW hard you try to avoid it, at some point you *will* end up with a broken heart. But that doesn't mean you stop playing the game. As Steve Ward puts it, "I believe in the Michael Jordan Rule—you miss 100 percent of the shots you don't take. So, if anything, if you're going to give up (on fantasy football or the dating scene) then why not just take more chances? You've got less to lose, so I'd say before you give up, give it another shot."

All of which brings me to the following story—one that combines improvisation, sports, and the pursuit of romance together in one neat package. As I mentioned earlier, I used to perform improv in New York City, and on one particular occasion, we were booked to do our road version of *Theatresports*, a show where five of us would split up into two teams (plus a referee) and each duo would perform scenes in order to try and win the audience's favor, in an effort to earn the most points and be declared the night's champion.

This particular outing was at Club Getaway, a sort of "resort of last resort" for singles in search of love. Now I'd never been to Club Getaway before, but it has its reputation in New York City. Located in the Connecticut woods, and affectionately called Club No-Pants, it is advertised as one of those "meat markets disguised as a summer camp for adults."

Now it doesn't say so in the brochure, but you know there's a lot of hanky and an equal amount of panky going on after lights out. After doing shows for kids in schools nonstop for the previous six months, it was going to be great to be able to get a bit raunchy on stage. In short, this was to be a perfect audience for us—and we were the featured entertainment for the weekend.

Our show was scheduled for Saturday night at 10:30, and due to the various schedules of the five of us making this particular trip, we couldn't get up there until 3:00 PM on Saturday, and we couldn't stay overnight because Lynn-Marie had a 10:00 AM flight on Sunday. "But that's OK," said Kenn, the only one of us who had been there before, "because they serve a 'fine dinner,' and we'll at least be able to get some swimming in."

We set out on the road from Manhattan and plotted a course for Club Getaway. The directions they had sent us were quite misleading, and although we should have arrived at three, we ended up getting there at closer to 4:30—but all in all, not such a bad trip. There was still plenty of time to go swimming and have that "fine dinner."

We parked in an area labeled Free Parking and proceeded on foot to the main office to check in. As we walked, an old grizzled cowboy drove by in a pickup truck. The man at the office yelled, "Hi, Slim." Slim grumbled back, "A-yuh" and proceeded to speed past us toward the basketball courts in the distance. The man at the office then turned his attention to our quintet and, even after we introduced ourselves, had no idea who we were or why we were there. He got on his walkie-talkie and spoke in some sort of indecipherable code, and after a few minutes told us to "go see Wally over at the Waterworks." It is indeed at this point that my suspicions were confirmed, as I looked in the distance and saw that the main office was in fact adorned with a wood-carved sign reading Community Chest.

Going past the many rows of—yep, you guessed it—red and green cabins until we reached the lake (aka Waterworks) we met Wally, who instantly greeted us warmly, gave us the run of the joint, showed us the theater (directly adjacent to the lake and right behind the basketball courts where Slim was busy unpacking large electronic things from his truck). Wally also gave each of us a handful of "Club Getaway Dollars," which look suspiciously like the ones you probably have in your closet at home, in the board game box next to your Scrabble set. Of course, to make them *official* you'll have to write CG on them with a green magic marker.

Sadly, Wally informed us that there was no room at the inn for us wayward travelers. We told him that we, at the very least, needed a room to store our stuff and to change into our costumes before the show, and that we weren't planning to stay the night, so whatever space he could possibly spare—it didn't need to be all that big or even have a bed or anything like that—would suffice.

We ask him again twenty minutes later, when it becomes apparent that Wally is drunk and has forgotten all about us. Another twenty minutes later and we are finally, at long last, sharing "St. James Place 5" with three of the counselors.

Now, a quick note on the way the cabins are set up at the resort. Each cabin has four bedrooms, numbered (depending on the cabin) 1 through 4, 5 through 8, and so on up to 17 through 20. There is also one bathroom within each cabin, predictably at this point, showcasing the Utilities logo on it. The only door in the interior of the cabin is the bathroom door, so "wandering" between rooms during the night is quite the easy task.

Now, allegedly, if you wanted a door for privacy purposes, you'd have to pay for Pennsylvania Avenue or, at the very least, Illinois Avenue. (We didn't see Baltic Avenue, but I'm pretty sure that was the cabin with the outdoor plumbing.)

So, it's finally time to enjoy our time at Club Getaway. We're told the lake is closed by now, so there'll be no swimming. But line dancing is still promised at seven, a fine dinner awaits us at 8:00, Slim's Square Dancing Extravaganza is scheduled for 9:30, and then it's us at 10:30 for our rollicking improv comedy show. I go off to play some tennis with Eris, while the others resign themselves to sit by the lake and enjoy what is left of a beautiful day.

We return from tennis to find our three companions in quite a cranky mood. We were about to ask why when we hear the voice on the loudspeaker kick in, "Let's hear it for our swimmers!" and as we look past the giant gyroscopic exercise device (affectionately called Jail), there were twenty or so campers emerging from the water after a brisk swim. Apparently, "closed" is a relative term here reserved for those who haven't paid for the privilege but are merely "just visiting." But hey, we still have that fine dinner to look forward to, so no griping. Line dancing was uneventful, save for the fact that the guy leading it got confused and called out the wrong steps frequently. Still, it hardly mattered, as few of the people in attendance could dance. Ah, yes—the people, the so-called swinging singles. If you were to see pictures of these folks, you'd be convinced the vast majority of them had lived there for generations and only now, after centuries of inbreeding, had opened up the camp to outsiders. Line dancing? These people had trouble walking the hundred feet from the tented dance floor to Go, the fine dining facility.

Now, if we hadn't been able to figure it out from the numerous announcements, it was quite apparent from the piñatas and all the red, green, and yellow streamers hanging haphazardly from the rafters in Go that it was Tex-Mex night. Well, that and the canned mariachi music kind of gave it away. We were seated at one of the two tables with a window view—the perks of being featured performers, I guess—at a table that seated eight, though probably closer to six comfortably. The five of us were joined by two women who we learn are "quite enjoying their stay at Marvin Gardens 5" and Ron.

Who is Ron, you ask? Ron is our "Table Captain." He's there to make sure we all converse and get along. Well, that's his job description anyway. It appears Ron is actually there to hit on the two girls from Marvin Gardens 5. Then our fine dinner is served: moist tacos, overcooked chicken, and undercooked rice. Um . . . yum?

To make matters worse, all the counselors burst in to the room suddenly, already drunk, shrieking "Tequila!" at the top of their lungs, dressed in flamenco shirts, and wearing sombreros. They weave in and out and around the tables in a staggering conga line, offering tequila shots to all who desire them. We, of course, cannot partake in the liquid merriment, as we must perform in two hours' time and need to have all our faculties in order to perform improv at our best.

Looking back on it today, I'm not exactly sure when we became aware of the wall of flame creeping toward us. It was definitely before the "tequila boys" did, I know that much. But there, outside the window, it was quite clear that several of the cabins were engulfed by a raging inferno and equally clear that between us and the cabins lay a nice supply of highly flammable sticks and twigs.

It was coming.

Quickly, Wally's wife, Sara, gets on the microphone and says, "People, please relax. As some of you may have noticed, there is a fire, but the fire department is already here. Everything is under control. Please stay seated. Remain calm. Stay here so we know everyone is accounted for." At least that's what I think she said. It was difficult to hear her clearly over the flamenco dancers running around willy-nilly outside, screaming, "Oh, my God! We're all going to die!"

Thirty minutes later, I see the fire department actually arrive. This is two Sara pep talks later. She then announces to the group that the fire is in Marvin Gardens 1 through 4. Anyone from these cabins is requested to come into the next room to talk. "Everyone else should stay put." Ron consoles our MG 5 tablemates, "Clearly the fact that we can see the blaze is still raging wildly, and the fact that your cabin shares a wall with MG 4 . . . well, that's no reason to believe that any of *your* stuff has burned up."

The next announcement comes soon after. "Ladies and gentlemen, the power is going to be turned off. This is a planned event. Do not panic. The fire department wants us to do this, since this may be an electrical fire." Sara has now accomplished two things: 1) She has instilled a fresh wave of panic in the campers, as those who were not near the windows now realize she was lying all this time about the fire having been under control, and 2) she has further intensified this fresh wave of panic in the campers, as they all now believe that their cabins might burst into flames during the night as they sleep due to faulty wiring.

Another half hour comes and goes. The fire is indeed under control. More words of wisdom from Wally's wife: "Ladies and gentlemen, thanks for your patience and understanding. You may go outside if you wish, but please stand under the main tent and don't wander. And may I please see anyone who was staying in Marvin Gardens or Pennsylvania Avenue?"

"Which cabins?"

"All of them."

Outside near the lake, it's quite chilly as a brisk wind comes in off the water. I see Wally for the first time in hours, jumping into the lake for a swim. Sara, finally having had surgery to remove the portable microphone from her body, quietly approaches us. "Do you think you can do the show out here?" We tell her it's pretty cold out and ask if she really thinks wacky comedy is appropriate right now, and besides still, there's *no* power and it is pitch-black, save for the glow of Kenn and Christine's cigarettes, and does she *really* think wacky comedy is appropriate right now?

She thinks for a moment, and I can actually see her thoughts—the wasted dollar signs she spent for us to perform tonight running through her mind. "All right," she reluctantly concedes, "we'll cancel the show."

That would have been the end of the day and the end of the story. It should have been the end of the story. Except the fire department was still putting out the last remnants of the blaze, and the only way to get back to our car was to pass their giant hook and ladders. Currently, they weren't letting anybody through just yet, so while some campers began an impromptu sing-along to the guitar strumming of one of the other guests, we stayed outside to drink the free beer being passed around and wait until we could physically leave.

It was just after midnight when the power suddenly, and without warning, sprung back to life, both startling and blinding us all. Sara rushed over, her "microphonitis" no longer in remission. Defying all temporal logic, she tells us, beaming, "I've just made an announcement in the theater. You go on in ten minutes."

What Sara failed to grasp is that trying to find a quick fix to a disastrous situation isn't something you can just snap your fingers and will into existence. Say you drafted 2010 American League MVP Josh Hamilton in the first round of your 2011 draft. When he fractures his arm diving headfirst on a completely unnecessary attempt to tag up from third base on a foul pop-out caught between home and third less than two weeks into the season, you can't just close your eyes, grab the best available free agent, and expect to get Hamilton-like numbers.

Instead, you're going to have to work to get out of the hole Hamilton's foolishness has dug for you. Maybe you'll have to trade away one of your better pitchers in exchange for a better stop-gap option in the outfield. Maybe you'll have to try to cobble together a few smaller deals to try to get back what you've lost.

In other words, you're going to have to improvise. As for the five of us, we were shocked. We were angry. We were tipsy, but we were still there. We had no choice but to go on.

We passed Slim on the way to the theater. He had just finished loading all of his electronic stuff back into his truck. Apparently, *he* would not be going on as promised. "Hey, Slim," we mumbled. "A-yuh," he grumbled back as he got into his truck and sped off. Oh yes, it appeared the road was now completely clear of any large red, hose-toting vehicles, and cars were free to go on their way.

The guests were filing into the theater, many of whom no longer had any other place at Club Getaway to go. Due to the fire, there was an open bar—"No need to use your Club Getaway Dollars," even if you hadn't left them in your cabin. I was drunk. I was tired. I was still a little bit in a state of shock from the events of the day. I don't remember much about the show itself or the drive home afterward for that matter. In fact, the last thing I do recall, before I went completely numb, was Sara's introduction.

"Folks, I know we've been through a lot today. If any of you can spare some extra toothbrushes, toothpaste, contact lens solution, a T-shirt or two, underwear . . . anything really. Anything at all. These people lost everything they had in the fire . . . And now, here to make you laugh . . . *Theatresports!*"

I'm sure it was a fine show, about as fine as the dinner, anyway.

9

Why the Founding Fathers Would Have Hated Bill Belichick

I AM AN AMERICAN citizen, and yet, I have a confession to make. I have never voted for a president.

Now before you get on your high horse and start talking about how "one vote can truly make a difference" or trying to guilt me over "all the brave men and women who died fighting to protect my freedom" let me let you in on a little secret: I've voted; I've just never voted for a president—and odds are neither have you.

The sad truth is that most people have no clue as to how the election process in this country works. You do not cast your vote directly for the president; what you do is cast a vote for an elector. Who are electors? They are the people who *actually* vote for the president. They are the only ones who determine who gets to set up shop at 1600 Pennsylvania Avenue. The founding fathers of our country did not want to have a president voted into office simply because they got the most votes. That may seem odd; but after all, in those early days, before twenty-four-hour news networks could provide nonstop coverage of the year-round political campaign, it was much more likely that each state would simply vote for their hometown hero, which meant the candidate from the largest state would almost certainly always win. That's not democracy—that's just an illusion of democracy.

It's a similar problem that arises with the scoring system many fantasy basketball leagues utilize because that system also "seems" fair, when it really isn't. In these leagues, players draft teams and set a starting lineup of players for the week, which then square off head to head in a bunch of statistical categories, such as points scored, rebounds, steals, and the like. Whichever team wins the most categories wins that week's game—makes sense?

Sure it does, on the surface.

But say I have Al-Farouq Aminu of the Los Angeles Clippers, and he plays four games in a given week. He scores 33 points, grabs 13 rebounds, and manages to nab 7 steals. Meanwhile, you have John Wall of the Washington Wizards, who posts 32 points, 14 rebounds, and 7 steals over the same time. Basically, we've got ourselves a wash in these categories, and that's ludicrous.

How come? Well, the problem lies with the fact that the NBA schedule is far more "erratic" than in other sports. In football, forgetting about bye weeks, every team plays once (and only once) each week. Not so with basketball teams—while Aminu had four games in which to compile his numbers in the week in question, Wall matched his output in just two scheduled Wizards contests.

Wall was *clearly* the better player in these categories on a per-game basis. The only reason Aminu matched him was because he had an extra ninety-six minutes to accumulate his stats.

To me, that's as unfair as it would be if the president always ended up hailing from the State of California, simply because people there cast the most total votes—and it's why I'll never play in a fantasy hoops league that doesn't use *per game averages* to decide who wins each category. You shouldn't ever lose your week's fantasy contest simply because the other guy's squad of scrubs got to showcase their "suckitude" twice as often as your studs had opportunity to take the court and shine.

Of course, the founding fathers did recognize that states with more people probably should be given at least *a little bit* more say in who wins than those with fewer residents, just not so much that any one state could have a majority completely on its own. So, as a compromise, the concept of electors was hatched. Each state would be given a certain number of electoral votes, based on the number of representatives they already sent to Congress.

As a result of this decision, if you went into your local voting booth in 2008 and pulled the lever for Barack Obama, you did not actually vote for Barack Obama but rather for "Adam Shapiro" or "Jaime Stoeckle" to be appointed as one of your state's electors, and they would have pledged to write down Obama's name once the electors met to officially vote for the president.

.   .   .

The Best-Laid Plans

In the founding fathers' original plan, as seen in article 2, section 1 of the U.S. Constitution, each elector got to cast two votes for president. The person with the most votes would be named president and the runner-up would be named as vice president. It seemed like a foolproof system.

That is until in 1801, when both Thomas Jefferson and Aaron Burr received the same number of votes, even though they were both Republicans, and Jefferson was the party's "choice" for president. Ties like this were to be broken by the House of Representatives, and eventually it was—a whole thirty-six ballots later!—when Jefferson *finally* was given the nod between the two.

Shortly after that the Twelfth Amendment was passed, which was supposed to prevent any future problems. From this point on, electors would not list two names, but rather designate one presidential candidate and one vice presidential candidate to be elected.

But even today, unlikely statistical anomalies could crop up: Neither Nebraska nor Maine follow the same rules for electors as the other forty-eight states, where it is "winner takes all." These two oddballs give two votes to the overall winner of the state and one vote to the winner of each individual Congressional district.

It is, therefore, mathematically possible in the Pine Tree State for a Democrat to win one district, a Republican to win the other, and for an independent third-party candidate to finish close enough in both districts to earn two electoral votes without winning either—similar to the fate of the 1981 Cincinnati Reds who finished with more wins than any team in baseball yet failed to make the playoffs because of the "split season" format (due to a player's strike) that awarded playoff spots to the winner of each "half season." The Reds finished second in each half and watched the postseason on television, no doubt sipping tea and shaking their heads in disbelief.

E VERY FOURTH NOVEMBER, as the country's map is lit up in either red or blue, and the networks tell you which candidate is winning, they are basing it on the assumption that the electors will vote for the candidate they have promised to vote for. Yet, here's the scary thing—they do not have to.

In fact, *on more than 150 occasions*, electors have not actually voted for the candidates that their constituency had sent them to Washington to vote for on their behalf. Now in some cases, as in 1872 when Horace Greeley died in the time between the election and the "official vote," it was at least somewhat understandable. But in 1972, Roger L. MacBride, a Republican from Virginia, completely took matters into his own hands, refusing to vote for Richard Nixon, and instead voting for Libertarian candidate John Hospers.

His punishment for making such an audacious move? None, really. In fact, the Libertarian Party was so pleased by this vote that they nominated MacBride as their own candidate for president in 1976. On an interesting historical footnote, MacBride also voted for Toni Nathan, the Libertarian candidate for vice president, making her—and not Geraldine Ferraro—the first woman to receive an electoral vote.

In fact, even today with twenty-nine states (plus the District of Columbia) having passed laws that require electors to vote for the candidates that won the state's popular vote, the penalty for not doing so is hardly going to stop the problem from going away. Although the laws vary, the only "risk" for going against the will of the people is typically a small fine no higher than Wisconsin's price tag on democracy: $1,000.

So far, no faithless elector's change of heart has yet swung the result of an election, but it's not all that out of the realm of possibility. After all, if only two of those who cast their electoral votes to George W. Bush had chosen to switch their vote—or more likely had abstained—whether due to the contentious recounts in Florida or perhaps the fact that Al Gore actually won the popular vote, then the House of Representatives would have voted on who won the 2000 election, and who knows how that would have turned out.

Given the current state of politics, is it really hard to imagine a few renegade electors in the 2012 presidential election perhaps opting to lend their support to a Tea Party candidate who came in a close second in the primaries in order to stir up the proverbial tempest in the teapot, rather than voting for the name on the Republican ticket?

Ethically, they may be bound by their promises; but as a matter of law, there's really nothing to prevent an elector to vote however they choose to when the time comes to sign their name to their official ballot.

• • •

Bush vs. Gore (2006)

Although determining a winner in fantasy football is nowhere near as important in the grand scheme of things as deciding who gets to live in the White House as commander in chief, it certainly behooves those who are taking part in the game to make sure the methodology of determining a winner is clearly defined *before* any controversy arises.

You'd be stunned to learn how many times I've received e-mails as the fantasy football season draws near its end that ask questions like, "We have a three-way tie for the final playoff spot. How do we decide who gets in and who doesn't?" I can't believe that the possibility that two or more teams might finish in a tie had never crossed these owners minds, but I am, of course, far from shocked that the teams now awaiting their fate have very different ideas as to what should be the deciding factor—naturally, whatever swings the pendulum in each owner's personal favor.

Which team was truly "better" throughout the season—the team that scored the most overall points or the team that beat the other head to head? The fact is that there is no one right answer to this question, just as there's no one method that will always work in declaring an outright winner in a comparison between two fantasy football players.

Case in point: the 2006 seasons of Reggie Bush of the New Orleans Saints and Frank Gore of the San Francisco 49ers. Who would you have rather had on your team? Well, that all depends. Certainly your league's scoring system plays a part in that answer, but even then the answer might not be so clear.

Without going too heavy on the math, in one particular league where varying points were awarded for rushing yards, receiving yards, return yards, touchdowns, and receptions, Reggie Bush's overall total for the season bested Frank Gore's by a total of 343-309.

In that sense, Bush was the more valuable player, right?

Well, maybe not. If you went week by week, Gore had a higher fantasy score than Bush in nine of sixteen games. Using this way of looking at the numbers, Gore helped your team more.

So who wins this debate: Bush or Gore? To paraphrase Bill Clinton, it all depends on what your definition of "wins" is.

J OHN F. BANZHAF III is widely credited for inventing a way of determining exactly how many parties in a particular method of voting actually have any true power. Say you have a small company with three stockholders who are trying to decide whether or not to make a certain acquisition. Owner A has 48 percent of the stock, Owner B has 47, and Owner C has only 5 percent of the stock. According to the Banzhaf power index, all three owners have the same amount of power in this company because *any* combination of two votes will produce a majority. Now in a fantasy baseball league where trades are subject to a league-wide veto vote before getting approved, one would think that everyone has equal power, since one team equals one vote—but that is not always the case. Suppose you are playing in a twelve-team league and want to get a trade approved. You and the other owner are not allowed to vote, and in order to avoid a veto, your league rules say you need at least five votes in your favor.

Well, would you believe that as few as two owners can completely control your fate? Say that a pair of devious owners makes a pact to decide between themselves whether or not any trade should be vetoed. They then bring in one other owner and convince him it is in his best interests to join them in a three-man power group. They tell him that the three of them will decide on whether or not to veto each deal, majority rules, and then the three will all cast their vote that way.

It sounds like a great idea, but of course, owner number three has no power in this group because as long as the other two owners have their side agreement in place, they will always have the majority. Now, expanding on this idea, the trio goes to two other owners and convinces them to join up for an unbeatable five-vote bloc. "We can block any trade we want simply by voting together."

But these two new owners have no real power either. The original pair dictates the vote of the third owner, guaranteeing a majority in the five-vote bloc, who will now all vote together. Unbeknownst to three of these five owners, they will decide the fate of every trade based solely on the whims of the original duo. Yet because they believe they have power in this arrangement, they are unlikely to stray from it.

Here's a chilling thought—what if a pair of Supreme Court Justices opted to embark on the same course of action?

Hopefully, you are not in a league with any secret cabal working against you. Even so, as long as the power of veto is alive and well in the rules, you may have a difficult time getting certain deals to go through. For one thing, many owners will veto anything that comes down the pike, simply because they can. To those owners, I say, if you don't want to play in a league where trades are allowed, then don't. But if you are in a league where trades are allowed, then at the very least judge each deal on its merits, and not whether or not such a deal might end up hurting you in the standings.

The other problem with trades is one of judging fairness. Many owners will veto a deal simply because it doesn't seem fair to them. For example, take the following proposed trade:

- Team A gets Mark Teixeira of the New York Yankees, who hit 33 home runs and drove in 108 runs, while scoring 113 of his own in 2010.
- Team B gets Jason Bourgeois of the Houston Astros, who had no home runs, only three RBIs, and hit a sad .220 in 2010.

Certainly a deal like this seems completely lopsided, and a deal sending Teixeira from the last place team to the first place team would certainly raise red flags. But what if the team giving up Teixeira was in first place and the team *getting him* was in last? Would that change your mind? It really shouldn't, yet owners will often look at an owner's place in the standings to decide on the fairness of a deal, even one involving players of equal abilities.

The fact is, though, that for a team in first place making the deal for Bourgeois might well win him the championship. Consider the fact that this owner might already have an insurmountable lead in homers and RBIs. However, he might need only a handful of stolen bases in order to grab a few extra points in that category and stave off any late charge by the second-place team in the standings.

Mark Teixeira, who has stolen only six stolen bases since 2006, including none in 2010, is not going to help that owner as much as dealing for Bourgeois will. In fact, making this deal in mid-September 2010 would have paid huge dividends, as the Houston outfielder stole five bases from September 21 through the end of the season.

Ethically speaking, there's no reason to veto this deal. But many fantasy owners, like politicians, have a "win at all costs" mentality and have no problem doing whatever it takes to get a victory, even vetoing a fair deal that both parties involved honestly believe will help their own team.

One of the most controversial strategies in fantasy sports is called "streaming." That's when an owner uses the waiver wire as his own personal minor league system, waiving several pitchers from his roster who have already put up stats for the week and signing a whole new batch of starters for a day, then cutting them and repeating the process. This strategy works wonders in head-to-head leagues where "counting categories" are used to determine the winner of each week's contest. After all, it's much easier to get more strikeouts than your opponent when you have 100 more innings pitched in a given week.

Certainly, rules can be put in place to prevent this strategy if a league commissioner wants to eliminate it from use. Limits on the number of transactions an owner can make in a given week, requiring an owner to keep a free agent pickup on their roster for three days before he can be cut, or caps on the number of innings pitched per scoring period all would do the trick.

But to me, even though streaming is legal in many leagues, that doesn't mean I approve of the tactic. After all, the point of playing fantasy sports, as far as I am concerned, is to beat your opposition by drafting the best team possible and starting your optimal lineup. I don't think it proves anything to win your week's game because you were simply the first owner to wake up in the morning and, as such, got to claim all the top free agents of the day.

I have the same disdain for a common fantasy football practice, where an owner who has a team defense playing on Monday Night Football, and a lead in his game, simply benches that defense and runs with an empty roster spot. The reason an owner would do this is to avoid a negative score from his defense, which might cost him the game. He'll happily take the zero and the victory.

Yes, if the rules of your league don't specifically prevent such a move—though I think all leagues *should* have rules in place to make this illegal—then you certainly *can* do it. But I think it's the coward's way out. To me, the point of playing fantasy football is to prove you can pick the better team for that given week and not to demonstrate your ability to start more players with later kickoff times for their games just so you can "see where your team stands" and then manipulate the final results.

· · ·

The Ethics of Bill Belichick

Bill Belichick has always been a football coach who plays by his own set of rules.

Back in 2005, one week after the Atlanta Falcons had listed quarterback Michael Vick as "questionable" on their injury report leading up to a game against the New England Patriots—a game in which Vick ultimately did not play—an angry Belichick decided to mock the system by listing fifteen players as "probable" on his injury report for his team's next game against the Denver Broncos. Included in that group of players were Richard Seymour and Troy Brown, neither of whom even boarded the team plane to Colorado.

However, Belichick's most notorious flaunting of the rules took place in 2007, when NFL security officials confiscated videotape from a Patriots' assistant who had been recording the Jets' defensive signals, in violation of league rules, which state: "Videotaping of any type, including but not limited to taping of an opponent's offensive or defensive signals, is prohibited on the sidelines, in the coaches' booth, in the locker room or at any other locations accessible to club staff members during the game."

Belichick did not deny that the videotaping took place, but insisted that he simply misunderstood the rule. "My interpretation was that you can't utilize anything to assist you during that game," he said. "What our camera guys do is clearly not allowed to be used during the game and has never been used during that game that it was shot."

Captain Loophole at his finest!

Commissioner Roger Goodell was unmoved by this lame argument and fined Belichick the league maximum $500,000.

No means no, Bill. No means no.

WHEN IT COMES to ethics and sports, golfers live on a different plane of reality than other athletes. At the Verizon Heritage Tournament in April of 2010, Jim Furyk and Brian Davis were tied after four rounds of play and went on to a one-hole playoff to determine the champion.

After Davis hit his second shot, he went to tournament officials and called a two-stroke penalty on himself and in so doing gave Furyk the victory. What was his "crime"? Apparently, during his backswing, his club barely made contact with a stray reed. While nobody on the course seemed to notice, Davis asked that they go to the replay to make sure. There, on super slow-mo, almost imperceptible to the naked eye at regular speed, the reed appeared to move.

And so, Davis was indeed in violation of rule 13.4 which prohibits "moving a loose impediment during a takeaway," something that nobody would have even noticed had Davis himself not spoken up. Compare that to Derek Jeter of the New York Yankees pretending to get hit with a pitch in a key late-season contest against the Tampa Bay Rays, and laughing about his deception afterward, and you'll realize that golfers are a completely different breed.

While actions like those of Brian Davis are quite commonplace in the world of golf, it nevertheless seems preposterous that golfers are asked to police themselves so rigidly. Most ridiculous of all golf rules is the archaic insistence that each golfer is responsible for keeping his or her own score.

Back in July of 2008, Michelle Wie was disqualified from the State Farm Classic. Had she cheated and put down the wrong score on the card? No. She simply had forgotten to sign it. Although she was in second place after three rounds of the tournament, she left the roped area outside the tent where golfers check their scorecards, and her fate was sealed—even though volunteers immediately noticed she forgot to sign and called her back into the tent to rectify the situation. Had she perhaps taken one fewer step, everything would have been fine.

Here's the kicker. The incident in question happened after the *second round* of the tournament. Officials apparently only learned of her "leaving the roped area" the next morning, when those volunteers spilled the beans. Before that, they had no clue that Wie had done something so "heinous" as to take a brief stroll before signing her scorecard. Yet, these same officials didn't bother to tell Wie she was disqualified until *after* she finished her third round, and of course, after they reaped the benefits of all those viewers staying tuned to the televised event to watch the popular teen prodigy perform. Nice and honorable these officials are, huh?

Are you kidding me? There are cameras covering each and every shot of the tournament from multiple angles. A worldwide viewing audience knows what every single golfer shot—why do they have to sit in a tent and verify it for themselves for it to count? That would be like having the Los Angeles Lakers winning Game 7 of the Western Conference Finals by two points and then asking Kobe what he shot for the game from the field.

"15 for 22?"

"Nope, it was 15 for 23, Mr. Bryant—that's a two-point penalty. The Lakers lose!"

No sports fan would stand for such nonsense. Yet in golf, nobody raises a peep. It's sheer insanity!

Certainly, nobody is endorsing out-and-out cheating, and of course rules should be in place to prevent athletes from doing what they shouldn't—but when you have referees on the field, you are supposed to let *them* officiate. Let them make the calls to the best of their ability, and when in doubt, you can have another official up in the booth watching the replay monitor to call down and let them know when they've made an obvious and egregious mistake.

If not, you're going to end up with more and more situations like what happened during 2010 World Cup qualifying. France defeated Ireland in a two-game playoff for a berth in the World Cup when William Gallas headed in a late goal past the Irish keeper. The controversy arose when replays clearly showed that

Thierry Henry had swatted the soccer ball down with his hand before passing it along to Gallas.

The referee didn't see the handball (though after the game, Henry did not deny his illegal touch), and there is no video replay in soccer. So even though the Irish side got royally screwed, there was no recourse. As FIFA, the governing body of soccer, pointed out, "As is clearly mentioned in the Laws of the Game, during matches, decisions are taken by the referee and these decisions are final."

Of course, anyone who has ever had the chance to check out video of the mistake referee Silvia Regina de Oliveira made in a Brazilian soccer match will wonder why instant replay wasn't immediately adopted by FIFA. In a match between Santacruzense and Atletico Sorocoba, a player from the home team shot the ball into the outside of the net, and all the players on both sides began their march downfield to await the goal kick to come.

While everyone was in retreat, the ball boy softly kicked a new ball toward the front of the net; and before the goalie had a chance to pick it up, it crossed the goal line. Inexplicably, the referee saw the goalie retrieving the ball and decided to award Santacruzense with the tying goal. Again, despite incontrovertible video evidence showing what actually happened, the result was allowed to stand.

Methinks the Laws of the Game need a good rewrite.

In the case of Henry's hand ball, first Ireland appealed to the French Football Federation, in the interest of fair play, to agree to a rematch. Since this was soccer and not golf, that didn't happen, and France gladly made the trip to South Africa for the World Cup amidst Irish claims of a conspiracy to ensure the highly ranked French made the tournament, at whatever cost.

Perhaps fans of Ireland took some solace in the fact that the French team imploded, finishing last in their group at the World Cup, failing to win a single game. One couldn't help but laugh during their match against Uruguay when Thierry Henry fired a ball off a defender's elbow and then turned to the referee to complain that he did not give him a penalty kick for what he believed to be an obvious hand ball.

The announcer's one-word comment summed it all up—"Irony."

. . .

Conspiracy Theory

Pat Riley resigned as head coach of the Miami Heat less than a week before the start of the 2003–04 season. Although he remained on as team president, he let assistant Stan Van Gundy take over a team that had gone just 25-57 the year before—the worst record ever for a Pat Riley–coached side.

Under Van Gundy, the Heat saw marked improvement, winning 42 games and making it to the second round of the 2004 NBA Playoffs. The following year, Miami finished the regular season with the best record in the Eastern Conference. Stan Van Gundy coached in the All-Star Game, and the Heat came within one game of making it to the NBA Finals. In fact, if not for a rib injury to Dwyane Wade, the team's leading scorer, they likely would have defeated the Detroit Pistons in that series.

With the Heat no longer a league laughingstock, rumors began to circulate during the off-season that Riley was going to fire Van Gundy, despite his success, and reclaim the head coaching mantle for himself. That didn't happen, but after an 11-10 start to the 2005–06 season, Van Gundy suddenly resigned on December 12, citing a desire to spend more time with his family.

Though all parties involved denied that Van Gundy was pushed out the door so Riley could grab the glory, the Heat did go on to win the NBA Championship that season, and they won their division the following year as well, though they were swept in the first round of the playoffs by the Chicago Bulls.

In 2007–08, Riley's Heat were once again the laughingstock of the league, finishing with a disastrous 15-67 record. Riley retired from coaching after the season—this time "for good" though again he stayed on as team president. Erik Spoelstra took over the team, making him the then-youngest coach in the league at the age of thirty-seven.

Two years later, Miami signed superstars LeBron James and Chris Bosh to team up with Dwyane Wade in the hopes of once again returning to the NBA Finals. Again, Riley laughed off rumors that he was planning on getting back to the bench, but only time will tell. And the conspiracy theorists have already written the ending to this story.

H ORROR STORIES FROM fantasy leagues where a commissioner retroactively changes the rules midseason due to some heretofore unnoticed oversight that coincidentally manipulates the win-loss records of the league severely in his favor are, sadly, far too commonplace. But why should we really be surprised?

Our country was founded by people like Elbridge Thomas Gerry, whose signature proudly sits six names down in the rightmost column of the Declaration of Independence. Although Gerry was the fifth vice president of the United States, few people have ever heard of him, perhaps because he died in office of heart failure at the age of seventy.

However, his legacy lives on in American politics today, as his name forever became linked with a particular form of unethical practice by government. The word "gerrymander" refers to a tactic where voting districts are redrawn into shapes that make no geographical sense but contain a certain constituency. In other words, the political party currently in power draws the districting lines for

the next election with the sole purpose of ensuring they will keep their majority.

The first known usage of the word comes from Massachusetts where, in 1812, one redrawn election district had a distinctly reptilian look to it. A local newspaper added a head, wings, and claws to the district's shape on a map and called it a "Gerrymander"—a word combining the then-Governor Gerry's name with the word salamander.

Unfortunately for Gerry, who likely had little, if anything at all, to do with the actual line-drawing in question, the word stuck and his name forever linked in the annals of history to political deception and unethical behavior.

So I ask you—how do you want to be remembered by the people in your league? Just because you *can* do something, doesn't mean you should. Yes, winning your fantasy league, especially one with a large monetary reward attached, may be important to you—but how much are you willing to pay for that success?

Food for thought.

10

Smarter Than Stephen Hawking

T HERE IS A cat in a box, and there's a very good chance it might be dead.

Now, before anyone goes calling PETA on me, let me explain. This isn't a real cat. It's part of a hypothetical scenario designed to help people understand the complicated subject of quantum physics. However, if even the idea of theoretical animals meeting an untimely end bothers you, we'll change the experiment a bit.

Former Major League pitcher and winner of 283 career games, Jim Kaat, is in a box. He's been trapped inside along with a small sealed vial of poison gas. Every five minutes, Kaat is asked to toss a coin in the air. If it lands on heads, the vial remains sealed. If it lands on tails, the seal on the vial bursts, and the gas is released into the box.

Now comes the fun part. According to the laws of quantum physics—which govern the smallest of all particles of matter like the electron—until somebody opens the box to check on the man they call Kitty, he is both dead *and* alive simultaneously.

If that doesn't make sense to you, you're not alone. Even today, among the brightest of minds our planet has to offer, the Schrodinger's Cat paradox, as it is more commonly known, has multiple interpretations, explanations, and implications. But where there is agreement is that in order for any event to occur, someone has to be around to measure or observe the event first.

However, if you're a sports fan, I can help you easily wrap your head around this complex quantum entanglement that even gave Albert Einstein migraines. I can even do it two words: "Armando Galarraga."

The then-Detroit Tigers pitcher was one out away from achieving baseball immortality. He had retired the first twenty-six Cleveland Indians batters who had come to the plate on June 2, 2010, and if he could get past light-hitting rookie infielder Jason Donald, he would become only the twenty-first pitcher in Major League history to throw a perfect game.

With the home crowd standing and cheering him on, Galarraga delivered the pitch. Donald hit a ground ball to the left of first base. First baseman Miguel Cabrera ranged over to grab it, set himself, and fired it over to Galarraga, who had sprinted from the pitcher's mound to the first base bag. As Galarraga caught the ball, Cabrera pumped his fist in triumph, and the crowd exploded into euphoria. Unbelievable! A perfect game!

The only problem was that umpire Jim Joyce called Donald safe.

Joyce was the only observer of this event whose opinion mattered, and in an instant, he had opened the box and seen a dead cat. Euphoria turned into disbelief and outrage. Boos rained down from the stands as Cabrera stood frozen in his spot, hands atop his head in shock. All Galarraga could do was smile weakly, as his back had been to the play, and he truly didn't know for sure at the time if the call was correct or not.

Video replay of the play provided crystal-clear evidence that the ball had beaten Donald to first base. Even Joyce himself, near tears for having cost Galarraga a permanent spot in the record books when he finally saw the replay after the game, admitted he had been mistaken. Yet none of that changes the fact that when the play actually took place, Joyce was the observer, and he had observed that Donald was safe.

That's the reality of what happened that night—and it's the only reality that counts.

• • •

Baseball and Time Travel

One of the greatest mysteries of the universe is that of time travel. Even the brilliant physicist Stephen Hawking has gone back and forth on whether or not the human race will ever be able to achieve some sort of mechanism for achieving the feat. And yet, Major League Baseball seems to have managed to travel through time on a somewhat regular basis over the years.

In fact, it's not too far outside the realm of possibility that a player may one day strike himself out. Don't believe me? Read on, and I'll explain.

When the Houston Astros and Washington Nationals started their game on May 5, 2009, at Nationals Park, the two teams battled it out for 10-1/2 innings before a downpour caused the remainder of the game to be postponed until a later date, with the score tied at 10 and with one out and a runner on first for Washington. None of the stats from the game were official because the game had not yet been completed.

Fast forward to July, when the two teams were transported to a completely different city from where they started. Before a regularly scheduled game between the sides in Houston, the May game picked up where it left off. Well, not exactly. In the interim, several players had been traded away or sent to the minor leagues while new additions to the roster, who had not been with the team in May, were now eligible to play.

In fact, Joel Hanrahan, who had been on the mound for Washington when the game was put on hold, was watching the game on television, as he had been subsequently traded to the Pittsburgh Pirates for outfielder Nyjer Morgan. In a bizarre turn of events, Morgan was inserted as a pinch runner when the game resumed and scored the winning run for Washington. Hanrahan, over a thousand miles away, earned his first victory of the season.

Not only that, once the game went final, the statistics for the game were retroactively made official for May 5, meaning that Nyjer Morgan scored a run for the Nationals on the same calendar day he also went 1 for 5 for the Pirates.

Now, imagine if Joel Hanrahan had been up at the plate with an 0-2 count against him when the game was delayed, and instead of being traded to Pittsburgh, he had been traded to the Astros. When the game resumed in July, it's quite possible that Hanrahan would have been called on to pitch for Houston. Of course, the Nationals would have been forced to pinch-hit for Hanrahan, since he was no longer on their team.

According to the official scoring rules of baseball, had the pinch-hitter struck out, because the count was 0-2 when the switch was made, it would have been Hanrahan who would have been charged with the whiff at the plate. In other words, he would have struck himself out. Even more bizarre, if he had allowed a home run to the batter, he would have been charged with the loss in addition to being awarded the victory. Try to wrap your head around that!

WELL BEFORE THE start of the 2010 baseball season, I spoke with Dr. Neil deGrasse Tyson—astrophysicist, director of the Hayden Planetarium, Yankees fan, and all-around nice guy—and posed to him the concept that the official scorer of a baseball game, an outside observer who determines whether or not a certain play should be deemed a hit or an error, was just like the observer in the Schrodinger's Cat experiment.

"In a possible no-hitter," I proposed, "until the official scorer makes the determination of whether or not the fielder committed an error, both possibilities exist in a sort of limbo. He both has a no-hitter and he doesn't."

Tyson was tickled by this analogy and let out a huge laugh. "Beautiful. I love it. It could be either, and in fact it is the other in another universe that could be, and often enough the other outcome does exist in the universe created by video replay. And if it's not a play where the replay is allowed to come into play, then the official scorer is it."

Of course, back then, we had no idea how close to clairvoyant we were being, but Dr. Tyson says that predicting the future in and of itself is not only possible; it happens all the time.

"We predict the future all the time in the universe because the laws of physics empower us to do so. You can ask me in one thousand years in Oshkosh, Wisconsin, on October 5 what time will the sun rise, and I'll give you the answer to within a second, and the only uncertainty is if earth were struck by an asteroid and it changed our rotation rate. You don't have uncertainty."

So, fear not, fantasy sports fans. Dr. Tyson clearly believes where the amount of available information is large enough, you *can* get an idea about how certain players may perform in the future.

"Where you get correspondence is where there's enough data to make predictions statistically. There are all these ways to measure performance which are entirely statistical, and one important correspondence between fantasy sports and how one uses statistics is the more statistics you have, the more reliable is the prediction you make from it. In other words, the more likely your predictions will follow the integrity of the statistics you've collected."

The main keys to using a player's past performance to predict his future outcomes seem to be the integrity of the measurements, as well as what we can reasonably derive from them. First, let's take a look at integrity. Can you be sure that the information you have is accurate when you have such a small sample size?

In Week 1 of the 2010 season, Arian Foster, a running back for the Houston Texans, rushed for 231 yards and 3 touchdowns. This previously unknown player was suddenly the toast of the town, based solely on this one performance. So when Week 2 came around and he managed only 69 yards on the ground and no scores, those who had suddenly sold their proverbial farm to trade for Foster were searching for the nearest bridge off which to launch themselves.

It takes more data than we can get from just one or two games to know for sure what a certain player is truly capable of. That fact holds true throughout the universe, as Dr. Tyson explains: "One common way we encounter statistics in astrophysics is if you make a measurement of some phenomenon. Now, you never know if the result of that measurement is the measure of the phenomenon, so you have to take the measurement again. There might have been some fluctuation, the current might have spiked in the power supply or a cloud might have passed in your field of view. You just don't know. So you take another measurement the next day, the next month, the next year, from another country, from a different telescope. And there will be variations in the measurements you make."

Tyson explains that if what you're measuring is actually something substantial, then the average of all those many measurements should approach the actual value of what you're trying to measure. Here's where the second factor comes in—that of what is reasonable to infer from what you've measured. Say David Wright of the Mets hits 2 home runs in a game off Cole Hamels at CitiField during a Sunday Night game of the week on ESPN (it's my book and I'll use my own hypotheticals, thank you very much).

Now, what can we glean from that? That Wright hits well against Cole Hamels? Perhaps. He hits well at home? Quite possibly. But what about night games or just on Sundays or in nationally televised games? There, the connection is a little less direct. However, if over the next two months of Sundays, Wright hits 12 more home runs, possibly then there is truly something there to be examined. Maybe there's some sort of other variable—something he eats only on Sundays, perhaps—that is factoring into things, or maybe the whole thing is just one big coincidence.

"Suppose you took 1,000 measurements and 500 are 'zero' and 500 are '100.' The average is 50, but the average is not telling you much," Tyson says. "It's not telling you about the behavior of the system. It's like the famous quote where they say the average American has one breast and one testicle—that's mathematically accurate, yet completely meaningless—a culturally meaningless statement. No person has that."

Well, Chastity Bono comes to mind. But all kidding aside, Dr. Tyson's point is well-taken; not all numbers are created equal.

· · ·

Blow Out the Candles

Sometimes, statistics are simply not intuitive. For example, Dr. Tyson and I both went to the same high school (albeit around a decade apart), but this is not all that surprising. After all, we both grew up in New York City, which makes the chances of this happening, all else being equal, about 400 to 1, given the approximate number of high schools in the city. That's not exactly an "alert the media" type of happening.

Dr. Tyson and I also share the same birthday, the 5th of October. The odds of this happening seem a bit more unlikely. After all, there are 365 possible birthdays to choose from, ignoring the once-every-four-year February 29 option which only complicates the math. What would you guess—around 100,000 to 1?

Actually, it's only 364 to 1, if we assume that we both had the same chance at being born on any given day of the year. Obviously, that's not a valid assumption, as I suspect there are a lot more babies born in the last week of September and the first week of October thanks to office Christmas parties and *Dick Clark's Rocking New Year's Eve*, but it's close enough for the basic math we need.

So how many people do you think you need to gather in a room for there to be at least a 50 percent chance of having one matching set of birthdays? Clearly it is much greater than 2 and far less than 365, where it would take astronomical odds for there to be no matches at all. Even though it seems unlikely to be the case, the fact is that with only 23 people in the room, you have about a fifty-fifty chance at having a match. And with 45 people, your odds of a cake-eating, wish-making pair have already risen to 95 percent.

The reason is because you're not just comparing 22 birthdays to yours, but rather you're then comparing another 21 to the second person's, 20 to the third, and so on, which results in 253 chances to make a match, not just 22.

Maybe this will help—consider the millions and millions of possible names you can give a child when he/she is born, and yet, how many of you in elementary school had a teacher who needed to add the last initial to a pair of students—say, Jason A. and Jason H.—in order to tell them apart when taking attendance?

Odds are you did, and even in the most overcrowded school systems, you probably had, at most, 35 kids in your class.

S TATISTICS, THE BACKBONE of fantasy sports, also govern our universe. The whole concept of luck is one that makes Dr. Tyson cringe. To him, it's all just a delusion we all create for ourselves. When things are going our way, we think we're lucky. When we hit a tough road, we're suddenly convinced that we're cursed.

"I see it as a flaw in the wiring of the human brain that we somehow cannot get within our deepest understanding of phenomena that you can have statistically independent events that preclude any sense that you're looking at some trend line," he says. "When people think that they are lucky—yeah, sure you can be lucky—it means that the statistics happen to be going your way. But often when people are lucky they'll say it was destiny or it was fate."

Dr. Tyson proposes the following experiment to demonstrate the way people fool themselves into believing they have a guardian angel of good fortune sitting on their shoulders. Line up a thousand people and give them each a coin. Ask them to simultaneously flip their coins. All those who get tails are asked to sit down and are out of the competition. (If it happens that a single toss managed to eliminate all the remaining contestants, it would be declared a mulligan.) Do it again and again until you are down to just a single person left standing. Given the laws of probability, this should probably take, give or take, around ten tosses.

"So the person who wins—what the press typically does is go to that person, if it's a lottery or some other thing and says, 'Well how did you feel about it?' 'Well, I felt a heads energy about halfway through, and I knew I was going to win.' And so other people hear this, and they start believing that either there is destiny involved or there is some outcome that a person can *will*. What they don't do is interview *all the other people* who thought they were on a 'heads streak' as well but then dropped out. There are too many of them, and they're not interesting because they didn't win—but in fact the person who won was not the only one who thought they were going to win. The others just don't get asked."

Indeed, what ends up happening is that because people only hear from the winner, it creates the illusion of luck playing a part, when in fact no luck exists. After all, there was 100 percent certainty that *someone* was going to win—just like *someone* is going to win your fantasy league. If it turns out to be you, don't be fooled into thinking fate was on your side.

A perfect example of how easy it is for people to overreact to so-called bold statements is one that irks Dr. Tyson to this day. In 1969, just a few days prior to Super Bowl III, the quarterback of the heavily underdog New York Jets made a bold prediction: "We're gonna win the game," he said. "I guarantee it."

"It's like Joe Namath, where he predicted he would beat the Colts," Tyson laments. "Well, he had a 50 percent chance of being right. Then he beats the Colts and people are like, 'Wow! He predicted this.' Give me a break! It's not like there were a thousand possible outcomes and he got the right one. All other things being equal, there was a 50 percent chance."

Surely there was someone on the Colts who also predicted his team would win, but since they lost, nobody bothered to follow up, since that wasn't as good of a story. It's the media that, intentionally or not, perpetuate the myth of destiny being something tangible.

"The media conspires to give the illusion that people are someone in control of their outcomes. Or, winners give the illusion, when it's the statistics that get you there—because they're the ones who tell other people what they felt or what their tactics were, when in fact it was just a statistical fluctuation that leaned in their direction."

• • •

A Baseball Conundrum

What is the highest number of consecutive batters that a pitcher can strike out in a single nine-inning game?

Most people will have no problem answering this question. After all, there are nine innings, times three outs per inning, the answer must be 27. Of course, most people will be wrong because the correct, and seemingly impossible answer, is actually twice that amount: 54.

A pitcher can actually strike out *six* consecutive batters in a single inning because of the rule that allows the batter to advance to first base, if it is unoccupied, on a dropped third strike by the catcher. Although the batter is not out under these circumstances, the pitcher is still credited with a strikeout.

So, a pitcher may fan two hitters, have the third strikeout "victim" reach first safely in the fashion described above, steal second to open up first base again, and have the fourth batter swing and miss on a dropped third strike with the runner on second advancing to third. Then the man on first steals second, which opens up first base for the fifth batter to sprint to when this completely inept catcher drops yet another third strike. Finally, with the bases loaded, batter number six swings at strike three which, mercifully, retires the side.

Lather, rinse, and repeat for each remaining inning of the game and you've got 54 strikeouts in a row, plus a general manager desperately trying to acquire a better backstop via trade.

THE FANTASY PORTION of fantasy sports takes on an element of science fiction from time to time when it appears to exist in its own alternate reality. On May 24, 2006, pitcher Greg Maddux of the Chicago Cubs allowed six runs in six innings of work against the Florida Marlins. At least that was the case for about two months.

In mid-July, the official scorer of the game, Ron Jernick, reviewed the play and decided to reverse his prior decision that Hanley Ramirez had singled in the fifth inning of the game, changing the call instead to an error on shortstop Ronny Cedeno. As a result, five of the runs charged to Maddux that night were instantly transformed to the unearned variety, and his ERA for the year dropped from 4.99 to 4.60.

But for fantasy purposes, once a certain amount of time passes, it is utterly impractical to go back and change past results. After all, where do you draw the line, especially in leagues where the priority to pick up free agents is often tied to the order of the teams in the standings at the time when the moves are made?

Say you do decide to go back and retroactively adjust Maddux's stats and as a result of that action, the standings for that day are changed. Don't you then also have to redistribute all the free agent moves that had been made that day, which may then impact the following week's standings and that week's player transactions and so on and so on?

It's a Pandora's box that simply cannot be opened.

The end result to this was that if you played in a fantasy baseball league in 2006 and you owned Greg Maddux and had him in your active lineup for the entire season, his ERA for your team was 4.41. Yet, on the back of his baseball card and for the rest of recorded history, you'll see his *real* ERA listed as 4.20.

Dr. Tyson is just fine with these kinds of freak inconsistencies. "You have to create your own rules because you're not on the field, so you can be stuck in these modes," he says. "It's like an experiment in physics. I was on a mountain getting data on the universe, and there was an earthquake, as there often is in the Andes. It's a geologically active zone in the Ring of Fire that encloses the Far East as well. So there was a power outage, and [when the power came back on] I started taking data and it was completely screwy, and it turned out that the prism in my spectrograph had shifted. So, what I previously calibrated did not apply because there was a different alignment of things, and there was a set of data that I was taking before I figured this out. And so there's data that is actually useless."

In other words, it's possible for something to unexpectedly and abruptly change your conditions, and you have to be flexible enough to live with the fact that what you thought was reality simply isn't the case.

The fact is, scientists still don't have an accurate theory of the universe, and until one exists, we're never going to get the "right answers" every time. But as far as fantasy sports is concerned, it's still far better to play the overall percentages than to go and trot out as many crazy theories as you can in the hopes you've found the Holy Grail of statistical analysis.

Dr. Tyson could not agree more. "If you have only pitchers with ERAs of 10.00 and batters hitting .200, you're going to lose every game," he says. "There are some pretty much guaranteed statistical outcomes based on statistical performance—you can call that a law of the game. Because even fluctuations—if the pitchers are *that* bad and the batters are *that* bad—good (performance) won't make up for how bad everybody is."

·   ·   ·

Another Baseball Conundrum

Can a defensive team get credit for a triple play without a single player touching the ball?

While it is highly unlikely to ever happen, the possibility does exist. With nobody out and runners on first and second, the batter hits a pop-up to the shortstop and is immediately called out (regardless of whether or not the ball is caught) because of the "infield fly rule."

While the ball is still in the air, the runner who was on first accidentally passes the runner who was on second and is called out as a result. In a final act of absurdity, the runner on second stops in his tracks to figure out what is going on, gets hit on the head with the pop-up, and is called out for being struck by the batted ball.

We may never see this play in a thousand lifetimes, but if we ever did, why do I have the strange feeling it would happen to the Mets?

D O YOU REMEMBER the classic sitcom *What's Happening?* On one episode, Dwayne stuns all of his friends by winning the local football pool week after week. Eventually, after they all combine their money into one large "can't lose" wager, he finally reveals to them his flawless system for picking winners: "I take the number of people who attended each team's last home game, divide that by the number of miles between each stadium, then I subtract the quarterback's number to get the score of the game."

As for determining the winner? That's simple. Dwayne went with the team with "the fanciest helmet." Of course, it was a completely flawed system, but the money he was able to win from it was very real. Results are the only thing that matter, and nothing else. So, really, who cares what mathematical voodoo the champion of your league performed in order to set his lineup each week? He still gets his name on the trophy, even if his methodology was complete nonsense.

Remember that sometimes, it is in those moments where we make faulty assumptions that the greatest discoveries are found.

For many years, scientists had collected data which showed that Neptune was not obeying Newton's laws of gravity. Clearly, there were only two possible explanations for this. Either Newton's laws were wrong—a highly unlikely possibility since they had been proven correct time and time again since 1687—or there was some unknown planet out there somewhere in the vast reaches of our solar system yet to be discovered.

In 1930, pursuit of this mysterious Planet X led to the discovery of Pluto, but as it turns out, Pluto was not large enough to be the source of the strangeness of Neptune's orbit. The quest to find Planet X continued on until 1993, when the pieces finally fell into place.

Apparently one of the numerous observatories that contributed to the collected data on Neptune had been contaminated when one of the gear mechanisms had been accidentally moved during a cleaning, and when that one set of data points was thrown out, all the mathematical equations suddenly all balanced out and Planet X vanished forever into oblivion.

Yet without the original mistaken calculations, we might never have found Pluto. Keep that in mind the next time you try out a new way of looking at the same old numbers. Yes, you may be building your entire theory on a foundation made of quicksand, but that doesn't mean you might not discover a hidden gem before the house sinks.

To put it another way, sometimes when you open the box, the cat is indeed still alive.

11

The Dark Side of Fantasy

A LONG TIME AGO, IN A GALAXY FAR, FAR, AWAY . . .
The greatest upset in the history of the universe took
place as a ragtag group of mostly kids, whose vast
military experience consisted of nothing more than
bull's-eyeing womp rats back home on their sand
planets, took down the Empire's ultimate weapon —
the Death Star, an armored space station with enough
power to destroy an entire planet. Meanwhile, in the
not so distant past, right here on planet Earth, Alec
Sulkin, a writer on the animated series Family Guy,
and the proud author of the show's hour-long Star
Wars homage episode, Blue Harvest, speaks with
your author about how this could have happened.

T HE DEATH STAR was destroyed for one reason and one
reason alone—cockiness. Darth Vader and the Evil Empire
simply didn't consider the need to truly play defense against the
possibility of attack.

Sure, the design plans had been stolen by the Rebel forces. So what? What could those small-minded individuals possibly gain from having them? After all, the Death Star was heavily shielded against the possibility of any large-scale assault.

What Mr. Vader and his friends didn't even consider was that a single one-man fighter could sneak in past the outer defense, navigate the long trenchlike grooves in the structure, and fire a direct shot into a narrow thermal exhaust port that led directly to the reactor system, starting a chain reaction that would cause the entire Death Star to explode.

Oops.

Alec Sulkin, like most kids who grew up when the original trilogy of George Lucas's *Star Wars* movies hit the silver screen, watched them again and again and again. He knows these films inside and out and is a huge fan of them. When I told him my theory of the Empire's defeat, he immediately hopped on board. "I totally agree, and it comes through when Grand Moff Tarkin is told that [his crew] has analyzed the Rebel attack plan," Sulkin said. "He's asked if he thinks they should have evacuation vehicles ready, and he says, 'Evacuate? In our moment of triumph? I think you overestimate their chances.' It's a perfect example of that cockiness."

Sulkin compares the final outcome of *Star Wars* to the time in world history when the first explorers went to the Dark Continent as part of the era of European empire building. "The first white explorer went into Africa and thought he could control everyone and then was bitten by a mosquito and killed. He just didn't see that that could possibly happen. He could control everyone with whatever he brought with him but didn't account for the tiny bit of their culture that would come and kill him."

Similarly, winning your fantasy league once you've gotten out to a big lead is sometimes more difficult than coming from behind. Why? Well, because far too often owners at the top of the standings won't take any steps at all to improve their team. After all, how can you improve on first place? Unfortunately, that kind of thinking can be catastrophic. If you have a chance to make a move that will crush your competition once and for all, you need to make it. Sitting back on your laurels and gloating at how great you are serves no purpose and usually ends with a one-way ticket down a bottomless shaft.

The Empire made this mistake all the time. Sulkin laments their egregious lack of effort at capturing Han Solo when they had the chance. "Basically they would have the whole fleet after the Millennium Falcon, and there would be five of those giant triangle cruisers and then they would deploy, like *three* TIE fighters to go and get him," he said. "Each of those ships must house dozens of those fighters just sitting in the hull. They should just send all of them, you know? There's no need to cut corners in that situation."

Going for the jugular in fantasy might also mean doing things that sound counter-intuitive. So what if you already have nothing but All-Stars on your roster? If your chief competition needs help at a certain position badly, and you have a chance to claim the best player at that position off the waiver wire and stash him on your bench simply to prevent the competition from getting better, you do it. The New York Yankees, the Evil Empire of the Major League, understand this principle better than anyone in all of sports. They didn't trade for Lance Berkman and Kerry Wood at the 2010 trade deadline so much because they needed these veterans. They did it because *they* wanted to make sure the other teams in the pennant race who *did* need them didn't get them.

Another time-honored fantasy strategy of playing from strength is the lopsided deal that goes against you. Send Kobe Bryant away for J. J. Redick with three weeks to go in order to help another team improve themselves enough to eke out a few extra points at the expense of the teams chasing you in the fantasy basketball standings. You'd never make that move at the start of the season or if your league has some sort of head-to-head playoffs to determine the champion, but otherwise, it may well be the best use of your resources as you hope to lock up the championship.

Of course, just because it makes good sense for a team in first place to make a deal like that, doesn't mean that it will happen. People simply don't trust a deal that looks too good to be true, especially coming from a team ahead of them in the standings—and sadly, in real life, Jedi mind tricks don't work. You can't just wave your arm and state, "This is the trade you're looking for" and have the other owner accept, even if it is, indeed, completely on the up-and-up.

• • •

Jabba's Through With You

One of the most important things to remember in fantasy sports is that you can't screw people over and expect that people will forgive and forget as time goes by. Once you get labeled as a "stuck-up, half-witted, scruffy-looking nerf herder," it's hard for the rest of the owners in your league to ever think of you as anything else. And if you do make a deal with the best of intentions and yet somehow, when all is said and done, the perception of the rest of the league is that you did something shady and that you're not to be trusted in the future, then whether it's true or not, henceforth that is going to be the reality, like it or not.

While ultimately how others perceive may be out of your control, don't do anything to help tip the scales against you. As Alec Sulkin points out, "The Dark Side gets a bad rap, but you are putting yourself in a bad place just by calling yourself that. They need a better PR firm. Like UPS and 'What can Brown do for you?'—turn your shit-colored business into a positive. What about calling yourself the Strong Side? Why not give that a try and see how the universe treats you?"

If you dress up from head to toe in black armor, and go around threatening to kill people with a single thought, perhaps it should come as no surprise when even your own kids end up wanting no part of you.

I F THE *STAR Wars* films teach us anything about fantasy sports it's that using manipulation to get the results you want, while it may yield positive short-term results, in the long run hurt you more than they help. If Jedi mind tricks were really the be-all end-all, then certainly Yoda's life would have ended far more pleasantly than we see on the silver screen.

"Clearly the Jedi have the worst retirement plan of any organization because when you first meet Yoda and you find out who he is and how old he is, and then you finally realize how long he's been this powerful Jedi," Sulkin opines, in an attempt to come to grips with a plot point that always rubbed him the wrong way. "He lives in the worst—it's just the shittiest place—and it seems ridiculous that he would *want* to live in that place. I just didn't understand why he wasn't living in a palace somewhere with people feeding him grapes. No, he's content to make terrible stew in a swamp where it rains all the time. He should have butlers!"

Of course, we're only privy to the story from Luke Skywalker's point of view. Perhaps there was far more debauchery going on during his "secret training" than we were led to believe. After all, he was having some pretty vivid visions in the old tree cave. Maybe Luke was merely keeping in line with the universal Bro Code—"What happens on Dagobah stays on Dagobah."

I'm going to briefly break those time-honored rules and share a story from the bachelor party of an old friend—with his blessing—and though nothing went too far out of bounds, I'll still be taking the step of changing the names involved to protect the anonymity of the participants.

During a weekend-long celebration in Atlantic City, "Conrad" was charged with the task of procuring a "performer" for the festivities. In fact, he volunteered for the task weeks in advance. However, that fact seemed to slip Conrad's mind until about one hour after check-in. So let's just say when he finally got around to handling this business, he didn't exactly get the cream of the crop.

No, he got Satin.

Satin, upon her arrival, informed "Bachelor Bill" that this was her "first time doing this" and that she was a little bit anxious.

Now this was clearly not some cute little role-playing fantasy she'd carefully crafted over the years—no, she was dead serious—this was her initial foray into the art of burlesque, a fact that became all the more obvious as she nervously laughed throughout her awkward striptease. At one point, she got so paranoid and self-conscious that she quickly covered up and asked, "Am I really fat?"

Satin put on such a sad show. She was far closer to Jabba the Hutt in terms of sex appeal than she was to Leia in the gold bikini. Before long, most of the room, save Bill and Conrad, quickly lost interest and turned on the television to get some hockey scores and prayed that a trap door would open up and release the monstrous Rancor into the room to end the whole fiasco.

Suddenly, on a dime, Satin's whole demeanor changed. Still topless, she no longer seemed so skittish as she turned to the group and squealed, "Ooh! Did the Flyers win?"

Sometimes fantasy and sports really shouldn't mix, and this was definitely one of those times.

Whether or not Philadelphia was victorious or not, I do not recall, but I can declare without any equivocation that those of us in attendance that night were clear and decisive losers. Of that, there can be no doubt.

· · ·

A New Hope

When it comes to fantasy baseball, there are many people who swear by the "traditional" format of using category-based season-long rotisserie standings to determine a champion. Of course, the downside is that, much like what seems to always happen to the real-life Pittsburgh Pirates, fantasy teams in these kinds of leagues often find themselves mired in the cellar in mid-May, already with no realistic hope of finishing in the money.

In an attempt to keep owners from losing interest and checking out altogether, an increasingly popular format is the adaptation of the weekly head-to-head fantasy football schedule to America's pastime. With a "reset" of the scoreboard each week, a team that gets off to a slow start actually has a reason to keep plugging away at improving their roster well into the summer months.

Whether you're determining the winner of each week's game by the team that wins the most categories, or your league has created a points-based scoring system where each player's daily performance translates into a single number—a head-to-head system offers no guarantees against a fantasy owner waking up as June begins with an 0-8 record, and no realistic chance of ultimately making the fantasy postseason.

That's why my vision for the fantasy baseball league of the future not only incorporates several of the current popular formats, but also increases the chances of having all owners still with a reason to at least be paying attention as August cedes the spot on the top of the calendar page to its old friend September.

A twelve-team league kicks things off in March with a draft and proceeds to play standard rotisserie for the first ten weeks of the season. At that point, teams are split into two divisions of six teams each. One division is made up of the upper half of the rotisserie standings, and the second division is made up of the teams in seventh place through the cellar.

For the next ten weeks, teams play head-to-head, two games against each of the other five teams in the division. Four teams will move on to the fantasy baseball playoffs: the top three teams from the upper division, along with the winner of the lower division.

This method rewards teams that got off to a strong start to the season by giving them—in essence—a fifty-fifty shot at the playoffs, while still allowing all twelve teams in the league to at least have an outside shot at the title when the All-Star Break rolls around, albeit a much smaller chance for those teams that struggled out of the gate.

All four playoff teams are now on a level playing field, as the scoring system shifts to a points-based format. After the first week in September, the team with the lowest score is eliminated, leaving three sides remaining. Point totals continue to accumulate as another team is sent packing with two weeks to play, leaving just two sides to battle it out the rest of the way for the league crown.

It may not be a panacea, but at least it does the job of ensuring that any bad feelings you may have about your team's title chances are put off for many more parsecs than it took the Millennium Falcon to make that Kessel run.

E VEN WHEN IT comes to your own life—the one place where you'd fully expect to have plenty of control over the ultimate outcome of events—sometimes things don't work out as planned. It was this realization that inspired Bill to come up with the rules for a new kind of fantasy game: "Friends Rotisserie."

Originally, Bill had intended to devise an elaborate system of points to be awarded in several different categories, each relating to the most important aspects of a twentysomething's life. Unfortunately, other than employment and perhaps "bad habits" nearly everything else fell into the same broad area: sex. So instead, Bill's concept simply devolved into a series of wagers—Would Taylor be able to keep his commitment to give up cigarettes? What would happen to Perry first: lose his virginity or get a job? How long before Carson and Grace broke up after moving in together? Things like that.

At one point, Bill had as many as twenty-five different exotic bets on the board, nearly all of which had some sort of time limit to their completion. The main reason being, of course, is that because these bets involved friends, in some cases "winning" would mean rooting "against" your friend's happiness. For me, though I did not look unkindly at those who did participate, I wanted no part in the kind of karmic kickback the universe might throw my way if I joined the ranks of this new "fantasy game."

More than that, I just wanted to avoid being put in an awkward situation. After all, what would you do if you had $20 riding on whether or not a certain pair of friends would hook up in the next three months, and there they sat at a party, all alone, getting a little tipsy? Would you quietly leave them alone and let Cupid's arrow take flight? Or would you try to protect your sawbuck by sitting down on the couch next to them and killing the moment?

It's at that point where ethical lines must be drawn, and it may be a tougher decision than simply deciding whether or not to start a running back who's listed as "questionable" on the injury report. At least, one would hope it would be a tougher decision—or else, what kind of friend would you be?

In Bill's defense, though, he never made any wagers on anything truly serious, like a medical test result. It was always something done in the spirit of fun, and his rule was always that once the bet was over, the person had to be told about it. Full disclosure, in fact, was the reason nobody's feelings ever got hurt because you knew that even if someone had put money against you finding a job in the next three weeks, they'd still go ahead and get you an interview for that open position at their company.

As Bill puts it, "It was just the thrill of having a little bit of competition added to something you would normally not have any control over. The spirit of these bets was positive. After all, even if you lost the bet, you also won, because it meant something good had happened to a friend." In other words, it was no more than an extension of the gossip that all groups of friends do when one of their number wasn't around that particular night.

Nobody got hurt. Nobody died.

Of course, some people have no problem taking fantasy formats to the extreme. There are a number of leagues where "rooting for death" is the sole purpose for playing. Competitions like the Lee Atwater Invitational Dead Pool are easy to find on the Internet. In this particular contest, for the low entry price of $15—and perhaps part of your soul—you can submit a list of ten celebrities who you think will die in the upcoming calendar year. Get the most right and you may well win the top prize, which for 2009 was listed as $3,000.

Incidentally, this is just in: Aquarium workers in the town of Oberhausen were shocked and saddened to discover the lifeless body of Paul the Octopus floating in his tank on the morning of October 26, 2010. No foul play is suspected, especially not from Lee Atwater contestants, as celebrities, as defined by this particular contest, may not be animals.

Of course, according to the legal disclaimer you would be disqualified should you be implicated in any criminal violation in connection with any celebrity you've projected for an early curtain call, so apparently there are at least some lines that are still worthy of not being crossed. But sadly, the state of the world today also dictates that said legal disclaimer is necessary in the first place.

In the interest of fair play, I contacted the folks at Stiffs.com, who run the Dead Pool in question, and allowed them to defend themselves from those who might be offended by their site and might even find it a bit ghoulish. The response from Kelly Bakst, commissioner and chief bartender, actually made a lot of sense. "In summary, most all dead pools are about predicting death," he said. "And while that does indeed include *hoping* for someone on your list to die, the focus is more on doing your research to see who might be likely to go in the coming months. Ghoulish? I prefer scientific."

In many ways I kind of respect that approach. After all, people are going to die whether these pools exist or not; and while you certainly could get lucky with your selections if you "draft" blindly, doing your homework and being more informed than your competition is pretty much rule number 1 of any fantasy league. In this case, it just so happens to take the form of watching a lot of E! instead of ESPN.

In addition, it's clear that Bakst and company are mocking the whole essence of celebrity more so than focusing on the macabre. After all, if Robert John Burck were to suddenly pass away, apart from the human tragedy involved in any death, it probably wouldn't even register as a loss to most people. However, if that same hypothetical passing were reported using his stage name, "The Naked Cowboy" then a candlelight vigil in Times Square would surely gather quickly.

Sad, but true.

•   •   •

Fantasy Zombies

What is a fantasy zombie? It's an athlete who at one time had a lot of value in his sport but had long since fallen off the fantasy radar and was left for dead. Then, without warning, this player "rises from the grave" and once again finds himself thrust into a leading role in his sport. Want a few examples?

Pitcher Jose Contreras went 15-7 for the Chicago White Sox in 2005 and even got some MVP consideration that year. Just a few years later, he went 5-13 with a 5.42 ERA and no fantasy owner would touch him with a thirty-foot pole. But when Brad Lidge got hurt in May of 2010, Contreras took over as the Philadelphia

Phillies' closer and with three saves in a two-week stretch suddenly walked the earth again.

Cedric Benson was a first-round bust for the Chicago Bears, who in his three years with the team only rushed for 100-plus yards in a game twice. After two DUI arrests, the Bears cut him, but the Cincinnati Bengals gave him a shot. Few people noticed when he gained 282 yards in the team's last two games of the 2008 season, but in 2009, Benson finished eighth in the NFL in rushing.

Old Jedi never die. They just turn into benevolent guiding spirits. But normally, when people pass away, they stay that way. And that's a very good thing because according to a report released by Canadian mathematicians in 2009, the chances for the survival of the human race if—and hopefully not when—an outbreak of zombie infection should turn the undead into an attacking army of flesh-eating ghouls are not good.

Their conclusion was not optimistic, barring an extremely quick and violent response from the living: "A zombie outbreak is likely to lead to the collapse of civilisation, unless it is dealt with quickly," the report stated. "While aggressive quarantine may contain the epidemic, or a cure may lead to coexistence of humans and zombies, the most effective way to contain the rise of the undead is to hit hard and hit often."

In other words, use the force, Luke. Use the force.

FANTASY PLAYERS CAN learn a lot from *Star Wars*. For one thing, it preaches the importance of being flexible and not stubbornly sticking to a proven-to-be-flawed strategy. Again, we turn to Alec Sulkin for his views on the subject.

"I thought it was a big mistake to rebuild the Death Star," Sulkin said. "It seemed like there was nothing new. It could have been something where they're remaking the Death Star, but this time, there's a force field around it, or there's a giant concrete exterior—space concrete, of course. It seems like simply rebuilding was not the way to go."

I won't even get him started on the fact that the Empire's ground assault was defeated by tiny twig-toting teddy bears. Epic fail!

The original trilogy is, at its core, a battle of good versus evil and teaches us that though rules can be broken, it is far better to win honorably. I've said it before, and I'll say it again, just because you *can* do something, doesn't mean you should.

For example, all Imperial Stormtroopers are genetically identical, having been cloned from the template provided by Jango Fett. We know that Jedi mind tricks only work on certain individuals, but we know that it does work on Stormtroopers, as Obi-Wan Kenobi demonstrates at Mos Eisley Spaceport.

Therefore, since they are all clones of each other, Jedi mind tricks will work on *all* Stormtroopers, and yet, because it is morally wrong to violate a person's free will, Jedi will not use this power for personal gain. Obi-Wan could easily have waved his arm and convinced at least a good couple thousand members of the white-armored simpletons to press the self-destruct button on the Death Star, saving the Rebels a lot of time and sparing a lot of bloodshed. Yet, wouldn't that have made him no better than the people he was fighting?

So, say someone offers you a trade on your league's website on Friday, but you don't see the offer until Monday, the day after the player he wanted from you shatters his leg in four places. Now, you certainly *can* click on the accept button. After all, he offered you the trade of his own free will, and had you accepted it immediately, he'd be out of luck. But that's not what happened and you know it. Accepting the deal now is simply the wrong thing to do and is sure to make you one of the most hated creatures in the galaxy.

On the other side of the coin, if you're the victim of such a bully, and your cries of protest fall on deaf ears, then it's better to find yourself a new league in which to play. After all, playing fantasy sports is supposed to be fun. Even though you may be in the right, you won't likely convince unsupportive owners to change their view of the situation.

In other words, I suggest a new strategy: let the Wookiee win.

12

The Thrill of Vicarious Victory

M Y FIRST YEAR as commissioner of my own fantasy baseball league was in 1994. I had pitched the idea to a few
of my college friends, and, with only a minor amount of arm
twisting, it came to pass that eight of us gathered together for a
National League–only auction. One of them actually showed up
in a seersucker suit and bow tie, in an attempt to channel his inner
Frank Cashen. As for me, I was proudly sporting a newly grown
goatee, just ahead of the facial-hair fad that would soon take the
country by storm. Upon seeing my "new look" one of my cohorts
said I looked "evil"—and so, after making sure I paid good fantasy
money on goatee-sporting John Smoltz of the Atlanta Braves, I
named my inaugural squad *Pure Evil*.

Meanwhile, approximately one thousand miles away, in West
Memphis, Arkansas, teenagers Damien Echols, Jason Baldwin,
and Jessie Misskelley were busy doing something far less enjoy-
able—namely, standing trial for the murders of three eight-year-
old boys whose bodies had been found mutilated in the woods in
early 1993. There was no physical evidence, no murder weapon,
and no motive for the West Memphis Three, as they would later
be known—nothing at all connecting them to this unspeakable
crime.

However, due to the grisly nature of the killings, the feeling in
the town was that it *had to have been* the work of Satanists or devil

worshippers—and Damien dressed in all black and read Stephen King novels. Jason wore heavy metal concert T-shirts and listened to "that kind" of music. To many, all the pieces fit.

Evidence was also presented that Damien had once checked out a book from the local library, *Cotton Mather on Witchcraft*. Ironically, this book was written by one of the primary participants in the Salem Witch Trials, and its actual content recounts the courtroom hearings where Satanic Panic had caused many innocent people to be executed due to their alleged association with evil spirits and other assorted demons.

But it had the word "witchcraft" in the title, and really, that's all the jury needed to hear. In fact, jury foreman Ken Arnold would later tell reporters that by looking in Damien's eyes "you knew he was evil."

Back in New York, I sat in my bed, mindlessly doodling ideas for a cool logo for my fantasy baseball team that ultimately consisted of a reaper's scythe dripping blood as the West Memphis Three were each found guilty, in two separate trials, on all counts.

· · ·

Giving up Control

Most football coaches are control freaks. They want to have a hand in everything that goes on in their organization, from player personnel decisions to the dress code their athletes must adhere to while riding the team bus to the airport.

While they aren't always given the power to make *all* of those choices, when it comes to calling plays during the game, there's no question that the proverbial buck stops with them. After the fact, the media, the fans, and sometimes even disgruntled players on the team are more than happy to play "Monday morning quarterback" and tell the coach exactly where he went wrong and what they would have done differently, but there are few people who would argue that those choices aren't the coach's to make.

Coaches are loathe to cede this supreme authority for any reason, yet former Notre Dame head coach Charlie Weis did just that in September of 2005. Weis had been introduced to ten-year-old Montana Mazurkiewicz, a huge fan of the Fighting Irish, who had been diagnosed with an inoperable brain tumor. Weis asked the boy if there was anything he could do for him and agreed to let Montana call the first play of the upcoming game against the University of Washington. He told Weis to "pass to the right."

Sadly, Montana died the day before the game, but Weis vowed to keep his promise. Notre Dame kicked off, and Washington marched down the field before Huskies receiver Craig Chambers fumbled on his way to end zone. Notre Dame recovered, meaning their "first play" would originate from their own 1-yard line—not exactly a situation where passing the ball was recommended. Nevertheless, Weis told his quarterback, Brady Quinn, to go with Montana's play.

Quinn threw the ball to tight end Anthony Fasano, who caught the ball and then jumped over a defender to gain 13 yards. The emotional boost that the team got from successfully pulling off the play helped to propel them to a 19-point victory.

Weis later said he had "no choice" but to call that play, but of course he did. He could have just as easily called a safer play and apologized to the grieving family afterward. When it comes to our own actions, we all have millions of decisions to make every day.

Here's to hoping the choices we make more often resemble Weis's from that day than not.

J ANE ESPENSON IS a former writer for *Buffy the Vampire Slayer* and has also written episodes for countless other shows including sci-fi/fantasy fare such as *Angel, Firefly, Star Trek: Deep Space Nine, Dollhouse,* and *Caprica.* What all of those shows have in common is an incredibly rabid fan base made up of people who completely immerse themselves into the universes created by the writers of the programs.

Espenson recognizes a definite parallel between the commitment made by these fans and those of us who play fantasy sports. After all, in both cases, we're investing ourselves fully into something—be it a group of characters or a team of players—that technically doesn't exist.

"I've seen (fantasy sports) played, and it's interesting to see it tap into the player's pride in the intellectual mastery of the study of a physical game . . . a way to *turn* a game of physical talent into a game of the mind," Espenson shares. "And of course once you've committed brain power to a project, then it gets into your envelope of personal pride. Add the competitive aspect and I can see how it would be all-consuming. You also have the nice feature for those of us who like to compete but not confront, that it's played at a distance."

This goes to the very heart of why fantasy sports works, I think. There's a very human need to be able to have control over our lives. We all actively surround ourselves with a support system that confirms, rather than questions, our own belief system. But in most cases, we don't have the power to take full charge of our everyday lives. We *have* to wake up in the morning in order to catch the train to make it on time to the meeting that someone else has scheduled for us in order to complete the project that somebody else wants done. If we don't, we won't be able to get that next paycheck which subsequently allows us to do the things we actually want to do, the things in which we do have the ability to decide for ourselves whether or not we will take part.

The draw of having active participation in events we'd otherwise have no control over is the reason shows like *American Idol* and *Dancing with the Stars* are consistently at the top of the ratings. The appeal of competitive reality shows where viewers can have a say in how the show ultimately ends is something that scripted fare—even the most popular programs—can't offer.

Fans of a show like *Lost* were never going to be satisfied with how it ended because there was never going to be a consensus among the core viewership as to what would make up the "right" ending. However, if the majority of people watching *So You Think You Can Dance?* believe that Lauren should beat out Kent for the top prize, then guess what? Lauren wins. There's a feeling of not only community, but also of empowerment that you get from playing fantasy sports which appeals to a part of our nature that we can't access by merely sitting back as a passive witness to events. Espenson, by virtue of being a television writer, actually does possess the ability to exert some control over the events that will unfold to these characters she's grown to care about.

"Well, that's why I became a writer, actually. I wanted to be able to make things happen to my favorite characters on *M*A*S*H**, *Barney Miller*, *Soap*—all the shows of my childhood. Of course, I didn't get to influence those shows, long gone by the time I got here, but I've been lucky enough to write for a number of shows where I was a fan before I joined the staff. And it really has turned out to be the best part of the job."

In a way, every show Espenson works on becomes *American Idol*, as she gets to spend her days in the writer's room "voting" on what should happen next. Of course, it's not a strict democracy, and the showrunner ultimately has the final say on the direction of the plot, but certainly, some of her ideas will shape the course of a show's ultimate story arc.

. . .

Dead, From New York!

Back in the dark ages when people actually had to spin a dial in order to make phone calls, comedian Eddie Murphy nearly caused AT&T's entire system to crash.

On April 10, 1982, Murphy appeared on *Saturday Night Live*, along with a friend of his named Larry. Larry was a lobster—a real lobster—and Murphy put his pal's fate in the hands of the viewing audience. He explained to viewers the then-foreign concept of calling into "1-900" numbers to cast a vote as to whether or not Larry would become his late night snack or be allowed to live.

Over the next half hour, nearly five hundred thousand calls were made, and by a narrow margin, Larry the Lobster's stay of execution was granted.

Of course, just because you tell people they have control over an outcome doesn't mean they actually do—as Murphy demonstrated the following week, for comic effect of course, by digging into a plate of boiled lobster and announcing that Larry's stay of execution had come to an end. A delicious, buttery end.

MAKE NO MISTAKE about it—teenagers have the capacity for great evil.

In season 3 of *Buffy*, Jane Espenson wrote an episode entitled "Earshot" that played upon this all-too-real fact of life. In this episode, Buffy is infected by the blood of a demon and gains the ability to hear other people's thoughts. In the cafeteria at her high school, she hears somebody think to themselves, "By this time tomorrow, I'll kill you all." Eventually, the search for the murderer's identity leads to nerdy outcast, Jonathan, who has brought a shotgun to school and is busy assembling it in the clock tower.

"Earshot" was originally scheduled to debut on April 27, 1999, but it did not air that day due to an event that took place just one week prior—the tragedy at Columbine. Even though we learn at the end of Espenson's script that Jonathan was not planning on mass murder, but rather on committing suicide, and that the actual would-be murderer was the lunch lady, who was adding rat poison to the mystery meat, the story was a little too "on the mark" given the horrific actions of Eric Harris and Dylan Klebold in Littleton, Colorado.

Espenson was glad the decision was made to postpone the episode until September. "My feelings, of course, were primarily about the people directly affected," she said. "[It was] an awful event. School shootings had happened before, of course—that was how we thought to even have this happen on the show—but the timing was very bad. I was relieved when I heard the episode would be delayed. [It was] not just better for the world, but better for the show. The show is intended to be funny, and that episode was not funny at that time. When it did air I watched it again and was pleased to see that the message came across as a very positive and relevant one."

While teenagers are very capable of doing very bad things and, therefore, should not automatically excluded from the suspect pool when a heinously violent crime takes place, as we learn at the end of "Earshot" it would equally be a mistake to jump to the conclusion that they are the *only* possible candidates to consider.

Of course, if your mind is already made up about something, it's nigh on impossible to dissuade you from that fact. For fantasy baseball players, the travails of Dan Haren are well-known. His reputation is that of being nearly unhittable at the start of a baseball season, but that once the All-Star break passes, it's time for you to send him packing, due to his propensity for a complete statistical collapse in the second half.

The problem is that the facts don't actually bear this out. For example, his career numbers for the month of May are almost indiscernible from his September statistics. Lifetime, through 2010, Haren has a record of 47-37 with an ERA of 3.29 in the first half of the baseball year. In the second half, his record stands at

44-37—with three fewer overall starts. Yes, his ERA is a bit higher at 4.07, but he makes up for that fact with a higher K/9 strikeout ratio from mid-July on. Yet, Haren will most likely continue to wear this albatross around his neck, and the bad reputation will linger even after a 2010 season where he won 50 percent of his decisions in each half of the campaign and lowered his ERA from 4.36 at the All-Star break to 3.91 by season's end. "Well, he only had a better second half because he was traded mid-season to a better pitcher's park," his detractors will argue.

Of course, the fact that he went from the National League (Arizona) to the American League (Los Angeles Angels) probably should have brought with it an accompanying increase to his ERA, given the stronger lineups he was to face in the AL, who utilize a designated hitter instead of a weak-hitting pitcher in their lineups. Yet the 2.87 ERA he posted in Anaheim, not to mention a nearly 40-point drop in batting average against, seems to tell a much different tale.

In the case of Damien Echols, the die was cast once the rumors started spreading that the murders were work of a satanic cult. In fact, given the lack of any physical evidence connecting Damien to the crime, leaning on speculation and gossip was likely the only way the prosecution would be able to secure a conviction.

At the time the bodies were discovered, one of the lead investigators in the case was specifically asked if there was any evidence of cult-related activity, and he firmly stated there was not. One month later, as the West Memphis Three were brought into custody, many of the local newspapers quoted onlookers (who declined to identify themselves) as swearing that all three suspects were known devil worshippers and had satanic tattoos. Several area churches held emergency vigils to combat the rising power of Satan in their communities.

By the time Damien's trial got under way, one of the chief witnesses against him was a so-called expert in the occult, who testified—among other things—that the *lack* of physical evidence left at the scene, such as there being almost no trace of blood, should be seen as *proof* of a Satanic ritual having taken place (presumably since Satanists would either drink the blood or take it home with them for use in future rituals).

That kind of twisted logic is akin to believing that aliens landed in your backyard last night because when you woke up this morning, everything looked exactly the same as it did when you went to bed—and that's exactly the sort of thing aliens would do when they flew back to their home planet; remove all evidence that they'd landed in the first place.

Yet, because local newspapers had run countless stories about the West Memphis Three being devil worshippers, the jury bought in hook, line, and sinker. Damien—and could a prosecutor looking to convince a jury that Satanism was involved have been blessed with a defendant having a more ideal name?—was sent to death row.

On December 11, 2010, Echols celebrated his thirty-sixth birthday right there on death row, still hoping against hope that somebody with the power to do something about it would listen to his claims of being innocent. And a big reason he still had hope was thanks to Johnny Damon.

•   •   •

Are You Not Entertained?

In the days of the Roman Coliseum, those gladiators who had been wounded in battle could make an appeal to the crowd to have his life spared. If the crowd felt the gladiator had fought valiantly enough, or perhaps if he was simply as hunky as Russell Crowe, they'd cast their support in his favor and he'd live to fight another day. The emperors would usually cater to the crowd's wishes—after all, the "shows" were there to entertain the public and keep the citizenry from revolting against leadership. So looking at it against that historical backdrop, the future of fantasy sports seems to actually be on a course headed back to the past.

Right now, variants on fantasy games extend past baseball and football to *Project Runway* leagues and the like or other similar competitions based on celebrity gossip—all the way to "drinking games" based on the number of times President Obama says certain key phrases during one of his speeches.

Even television writers, whose own works are often the subject of these unintended forms of viewer participation, I surmise, are not immune to adding this little something extra to add to the otherwise passive experience of watching the boob tube. Jane Espenson cops to being guilty as charged: "We actually had an elaborate betting system among some of the *Buffy* writers one year over the outcome of a season of *The Amazing Race*. Fun! But is this a trend? It does feel a little Roman Coliseum-ish to me, like elaborate bets on unlikely events has been a pastime for a long time.

"What's changed, I suppose is that we can [now] find others online who want to compete, and can observe more of the world at the same time, finding more things on which to bet. I guess if we trace this to a conclusion, we end up with everyone watching everyone else and simultaneously being the bettor in one transaction and the person whose behavior is being wagered on in another transaction. A *Truman Show* in which Truman is also watching the world."

In fact, the future that Espenson forecasts has already started to take shape, thanks in no small part to former *Buffy* cast member, Seth Green. Green (as executive producer) recently completed the first season of an online series called *Control TV*, where a "subject" agrees to have his life broadcast over the Internet for six weeks and have all of his decisions—what to eat, what to wear, what pet to buy, who to date, what job to accept—determined by audience vote. As the public gets more and more comfortable with both controlling and being controlled, it's not too big a leap to expect that someday in the not-too-distant future, a tech-savvy owner of a major sports team will dispense with his high-priced coaches altogether and simply let the fans vote on what their team does next on the field—what plays get called, what players get benched, even who gets traded to another team.

I fear for the day when the line between fantasy and reality finally disappears, and hope that we never get there because the next step down that slippery slope involves murder trials being aired as if they were game shows, with verdicts handed down based on the whims of a live studio audience. Once we start handing out parting gifts to contestants in the form of a trip to the electric chair rather than a trip to Hawaii, we've reached the point of no return.

How about you, what do you think? Shall we put it to a vote?

T O SAY LIVING in prison is a difficult existence would be an understatement, especially on death row, and after nearly a dozen years behind bars and seeing appeal after appeal for a new trial be denied, Damien was beginning to break down. His health was deteriorating, and suicide didn't seem like such a bad idea.

That's when a miracle happened. The Boston Red Sox came back from a 3-0 series deficit against the New York Yankees and won the American League Championship Series four games to three. It was the first time in Major League Baseball history that a team had won a seven-game series after losing the first three games.

As Damien wrote in a short essay entitled *Bottom of the Ninth*, Johnny Damon—his favorite player—restored his sanity. Although Damien would not consider himself a sports fan in general, baseball always spoke to him, especially the idea of a man standing all alone trying desperately to prevail over those who would keep him from "reaching home."

"I've never attended a professional game or played little league," Echols told me. "The closest I ever came was in gym class. I come from a very poor family. There was no money for things like baseball. What I like most [about baseball] is the comforting aspect; it feels like home, a security blanket, and it's soothing. It's the opposite of every other sport; people are screaming and cheering the whole time. With baseball everything is laid back. It is said that baseball is a game of anticipation, but for me, it's the long, soothing lulls that I like."

You think *you* live and die with your favorite baseball team? When Johnny Damon made his Major League debut at the age of twenty-one with the Kansas City Royals in 1995, Damien—only one year younger than the man who would become his salvation—had already been incarcerated for close to two years. And yet it was by living vicariously through Damon's exploits, by listening to as many games as he could, that Damien was able to find some solace during the times when he had "reached the very bottom of hopelessness."

If the Boston Red Sox could end decades of frustration when everything seemed to be stacked against them, and they could finally achieve the ultimate victory, perhaps there was still light at the end of the tunnel for Damien Echols as well.

In November of 2010, after over seventeen years of proclaiming their innocence, the Arkansas Supreme Court finally gave the West Memphis Three some real reason for hope. DNA evidence from the crime scene—which not only exonerates the trio but also may well implicate the stepfather of one of the victims—was finally deemed to be important enough to schedule a hearing on whether or not a new trial was warranted. The ruling was unanimous.

· · ·

Once More, With Feeling

After some thought, Jane Espenson offered up an intriguing concept that what people who play fantasy sports are really doing is actually a form of writing.

"Fantasy players are creating narratives and arcs for themselves and their teams," Espenson said. "It's like their own homemade sports movie, like *Friday Night Lights*. It's one of the most satisfying script structures—the little scrappy team led by a visionary who sees talent where others don't. His or her leadership guides the team through small victories and major setbacks until they find themselves overmatched but determined to go out with class. Against all odds they either win or, in the case of Rocky Balboa, lose with heart having won a greater victory. The fantasy player doesn't actually control the players, but they control the choices."

Espenson likens it to the difference between being the director of a show versus being the editor. The editor has no control over the footage that they ultimately have to work from, but by piecing the fruits of the director's labor in a particular order of their own choosing, they can completely alter the story's plot or tone—and they can do so without ever having been present for a single take.

Fantasy owners may not ever meet the athletes who make up their teams. They may not even go to a game in person. But they can still shape the course of their team's journey and are ultimately (perhaps) more in control of how the story of their fantasy season ends than the players themselves.

T HROUGHOUT THIS BOOK, I've talked about topics ranging from faith, Favre, and finance to politics, Pujols, poetry, and even a psychic octopus. I've tried to show how fantasy sports is more than just a "silly little game" and in fact can teach you far more about the world around us and the nature of human behavior and interaction than meets the eye.

I do take fantasy sports very seriously, but at the same time I also recognize that its primary purpose is that of being a diversion—something to help provide those who participate in leagues around the world with an outlet to escape from the stress of reality, at least for a short time. By living vicariously through the exploits of these athletes whom we admire for their abilities on the playing field, we can share in the thrill of their victories, without having to truly risk suffering too much in the way of the agony of their defeats.

But while fantasy sports may have begun as a lighthearted diversion, to many of its participants winning or losing is no laughing matter. And as a professional fantasy sports expert, doling out advice on a daily basis for ESPN.com, I have learned one basic and inescapable truth about my job: people take what I say very seriously. When asked whether Player X or Player Y would be better to place in their fantasy lineup on a given day, I am expected to be unfailingly correct in my advice.

On more than one occasion, I've made the wrong call—and on a few occasions received veiled (and not-so-veiled) anonymous threats from readers as a result. But what's the worst thing that has resulted from my mistakes—your imaginary team lost an imaginary game? Really? Is that such a big deal in the grand scheme of things? Have we truly forgotten that fantasy sports are supposed to be fun?

And it goes beyond just fantasy sports. For those of you out there who get far too worked up when your favorite team loses a big game, or in response to other things on television that don't go the way you want—I'm talking about you, guy who shoots out his television set after Bristol Palin advances to the next round of

Dancing with the Stars —may I remind you that there are far more important things to get upset about.

There are many advocates for the West Memphis Three out there, including celebrities like Johnny Depp, Jack Black, Eddie Vedder of Pearl Jam, and Natalie Maines of the Dixie Chicks. They've all spoken out in support of Damien, Jason, and Jessie. Many thousands of others don't have that kind of voice, but they've bought T-shirts or some bumper stickers in support of the cause.

When the day comes that the West Memphis Three are finally released—and count me among the hopeful that the day does eventually come—their supporters will likely feel a sense of personal victory and celebrate the news as if they themselves were the ones whose very lives were hanging in the balance.

On the surface, having that much invested in the events of someone else's life may seem a bit sad. After all, if the "best news you've heard all week" has something to do with Jennifer Aniston's love life, I'd say you need to take an inventory of your own affairs. Yet, at the same time, nobody has a bigger stake in the ultimate resolution of this story than does Damien, and it seems he has the least amount of control over whether or not he goes free.

Without all these other people becoming so heavily invested in his fate, constantly shining the spotlight in his direction, perhaps he would have felt the sting of the executioner's needle years ago.

"The people in the audience at a home game are like an extra player on the team," says Echols. "You feed on the audience's energy. It's the same thing in this case. Many times it's the only thing that keeps us going. It makes a tangible difference. People are watching, paying attention. They *should* feel a sense of victory when this is over. They have directly participated."

So perhaps the greatest thing that fantasy sports can teach us is how to feel.

It may not matter in the grand scheme of things if your fantasy football team makes the playoffs or not, but if by experiencing that minor disappointment it makes you understand what it's like to suffer a loss—even a loss as relatively insignificant as this—then maybe you'll be a bit more prepared to show compassion to others who have truly fallen on hard times.

Maybe, just maybe, playing fantasy sports can make us better people in the long run—or maybe that's just fantasy—and if so, then perhaps I've succeeded in explaining the world a lot more accurately than I thought I would be able to when I started writing this book.

But like Damien Echols, I'll continue to hope.

· · ·

EPILOGUE

T O FANTASY BASEBALL fans all over the world, there are four words that trigger a groundswell of emotion like no other phrase could muster. Those words are: "Pitchers and catchers report." That simple sentence, which typically appears in the sports section of newspapers and on the Internet in early February, indicates the official start of Spring Training—and as such, after a long winter's hibernation, the time to prepare for the next season's fantasy draft has arrived.

There is no time of the year more full of optimism for the fantasy sports aficionado than that run up to their league's Draft Day, which typically tries to coincide as closely as possible to the actual Opening Day, so as to avoid any late-breaking news of injuries that would cripple a fantasy team's chance at winning before a single pitch has been thrown. For the next few weeks, statistics will be analyzed, rankings of players will be made, lists of sleepers will be created, and all in the hope that once the draft is done, there will be no doubt that "my roster" has what it takes to destroy the rest of the competition.

Truth be told, it's very hard to draft a roster that will—left to stand pat all season long—outscore all the others.

- Players get hurt.
- Players you expected to be studs fail to live up to the lofty expectations.
- Players you passed on because you thought they paled in comparison to their peers suddenly have a career year for some other owner in your league.

In order to truly field a competitive roster, you're going to have to do some in-season tinkering. And here's where the true challenge comes into play and confirmation bias once again rears its ugly head.

Say you've drafted a pitcher in the first round and he starts the season very poorly. In fact, let's say in his first start of the year, he allows 10 runs in three innings. To some owners, that's already more than enough reason to cut him on the spot or trade him away for some other pitcher who threw a three-hit shutout in his season debut. Most owners, however, are willing to give the pitcher a one-time mulligan. But after a second poor start, the sweat already begins to form on fantasy owners' brows in earnest. How could this alleged ace be doing so poorly?

The truth of the matter is that if this pitcher had been selected with their last pick of the draft, cutting him would be of no consequence. Because no real expectations were attached with somebody you selected that late in the proceedings. If they perform poorly, there's no devil on your shoulder telling you that you should hang on to this guy just in case he turns it around. But, when we're talking a first-rounder, the wheels start to spin:

> I drafted this guy because I thought he would win 20 games and he's been just horrible! I can't get rid of him because if I do and he ends up winning 20 games, I'll look like an idiot. But, if I keep him and he ends up losing 20 games, I'll also look like an idiot. Maybe I should trade him now for that pitcher some other guy drafted in the sixth round? I didn't think he'd do much, but he's already started the season 2–0.

The problem with this line of thinking is that if all of your research led you to believe on Draft Day that this guy would win 20 games over the course of an entire season, just because he's lost his first two games, it doesn't mean you were wrong. It's such a small sample size to begin with, and on top of that, you also expected him to lose a handful of games along the way. If you trust your ability to assess talent, then the fact that he lost his first two games actually makes him MORE valuable the rest of the season, since he already has two bad starts out of the way.

Conversely, if you're suddenly of the opinion that your talent assessment skills are flawed, then how can you possibly think that you're in any position to judge the proper return value, should you decide to try and get out from this first round albatross in the first place?

Compounding the problem is that, even if you do decide that it's better to switch horses midstream and pursue that "over-achieving sixth-rounder" you're suddenly coveting, there's no reason to expect that you'll get him. After all, that other owner is probably overjoyed that his sixth-rounder is doing far better than he'd hoped. Why would he ever even consider trading him for your underachieving first rounder?

It's that darn confirmation bias that gets us every time. Your first rounder could have the exact same statistics as a player you drafted in Round 15, and you'd be over the moon with the success of one, while lamenting the troubles of the other . . . even though they have achieved the exact same level of success. That's a "you" problem, and it's a blind spot we all simply have. Once we've made up our minds about something, from that point on, we only judge new information as it relates to that starting point, regardless of how illogical it might be to someone considering that problem with all the current information for the very first time.

· · ·

On Wednesday, August 17, 2011, the hardcover version of this book was released. Two days later, on the morning of Friday, August 19, after all those years in prison, Damien Echols, Jason Baldwin, and Jesse Misskelley were released—but not without a ton of controversy.

The "West Memphis Three" were allowed to go free, but only after entering what is known as an Alford Plea. In this rarely-exercised bit of judicial mumbo-jumbo, the state of Arkansas was willing to let these men out of jail, but only if they agreed to plead guilty to the crimes of which they were accused. However, as part of such an agreement, the defendants were allowed to continue to proclaim their innocence.

If this "I'm guilty but I did not do it" plea makes little sense to you, then you're not alone. What it basically amounts to is that the state did not truly believe that a new trial would necessarily guarantee another guilty verdict in light of all the publicity the case had garnered over the years, and in order to spare taxpayers the expense of such a trial, they were willing to settle things once and for all with the West Memphis Three. By pleading guilty, any chance of a lawsuit for wrongful imprisonment or other judicial misconduct goes out the window as well, but given the alternative—more time spent in jail without the guarantee that new trial would indeed get Damien off of Death Row—there really was no other option.

Unfortunately, by pleading guilty, not only does the state get to say they were right all along, but they also don't have to do any further investigating into trying to figure out who was really responsible for the deaths of those three boys twenty years ago. The West Memphis Three are free, but they have yet to be exonerated. And in fact, based upon public reaction—while there seems to be unanimous agreement that justice was not served by this deal—there nevertheless is a huge divide in exactly what people mean when they say that. Anybody who was already convinced of the guilt of the West Memphis Three is now outraged that the state has allowed murderers to walk free.

And those, like myself, who believe the whole prosecution was a sham from the get-go are left scratching our heads as to how long it took for these innocent men to go free, as well as why the state can't seem to wrap its head around the fact that they've been wrong for so long.

But for all the parties involved in the original trial—from the police to the district attorney, to the judge and the jury—Damien was their first round draft pick. Come hell or high water, they're not ever going to be able to admit even the remotest possibility that they might have been in error, and they have no intention of ever trading him away for someone who's guilt they didn't invest nearly as much time or effort in, even if the circumstantial evidence pointing to someone else is just as strong, if not far stronger.

．　．　．

On the day that my book first came out, I wrote to Lorri Davis, unaware at the time that she was already en route to Arkansas to welcome Damien back into the world of the unincarcerated:

> *By way of thanking you for helping me out with the project, I wanted to send a copy of my book to you guys. I know there are rules about sending things to Damien, so I wanted to find out where I can at least get one into your hands . . . and perhaps you will be allowed to give it to him.*

> *Thanks again so much—I've started to hear back from a few people who have read the book already and one of the first things they've all asked me about is the status of the West Memphis Three, so hopefully the support continues to grow.*

> *All the best in the fight for justice, AJ*

Of course, caught up in the whirlwind of the days and weeks and months that followed, I did not hear back from them . . . at least, not until January of 2013, when Lorri and Damien left tickets for me to see a screening of the film *West of Memphis*, a new documentary about the case. After the movie was over, a rapt audience got to hear a short question and answer session with the guests of honor.

And once that was completed, I got to shake Damien's hand and personally give him a copy of my book.

Do I believe in hope? Yes, I most certainly do.

ACKNOWLEDGMENTS

WRITING A BOOK is something anyone can do by themselves. Getting a book published, on the other hand, requires the efforts of a whole slew of people, and I was lucky enough to have "drafted" a fantasy team that was able to turn my dream into a reality.

To my supportive family and friends—there are too many names to mention here. They are the ones who do it because they want to and not because they have to. To my beautiful wife, Sara, who was always able to keep my spirits up, especially when the process bogged down and I was beginning to doubt myself. I hope she knows I am her biggest fan. To my son, Xander, who in his youthful, constant quest for knowledge always challenges me to look at and explain things in new ways.

To my ESPN family for always setting the bar a little bit higher, forcing me to constantly become better at my craft. To Tristan Cockcroft, Eric Karabell, Christopher Harris, Jason Grey, and Stephania Bell. To Pierre Becquey, Brendan Roberts, James Quintong, and Keith Lipscomb. To Nate Ravitz, Rob King, Steve Wulf, and Gary Hoenig for their generosity.

To Matthew Berry, whose picture should take up permanent residence in the dictionary next to the definition of the word "loyalty." The list of people for whom I would wake up at four thirty on a Sunday morning—in the middle of a Syracuse snowstorm—

just so I can be filmed getting beaten to a pulp while wearing a giant papier-mâché fish head? That list has but one name.

To my agent, Jud Laghi, for helping bring this book into existence out of the endless jumble of ideas in my head. To Christy Fletcher, for being so supportive early on and for being so instrumental in the marriage of agent and writer.

To my editor, Mark Weinstein, Publisher Tony Lyons, and all of the gang at Skyhorse Publishing, the final "free-agent signing" that pushed us over the top and into the playoffs.

To each and every one of the people who graciously allowed themselves to be interviewed for this book, as well as the people behind the scenes who helped facilitate the connections, especially Elizabeth Stachow at the Hayden Planetarium and Beth Morris of Rogers & Cowan. An extreme debt of gratitude also goes to Lonnie Soury and Lorri Davis-Echols for their generosity of time and effort.

I also want to thank Sam Walker, Nando DiFino and Susie Felber, as well as all of the members of the Doug Logan League, both past and present.

Finally to all of the teachers who had a lasting impact on my life, particularly those who helped give this shy kid the confidence to find his voice in the world. To Gayle Kaplan, Raizella Mandel, Barbara Miller, Kate Andrews, and Ron Hastings. Thank you.

About the Author

Photo Credit: Caroline Twohill

AJ MASS IS a professional Fantasy Sports Analyst, working for ESPN.com, the most highly trafficked sports website on the Internet. Born and raised in Flushing, New York, within walking distance of Shea Stadium, he earned his degree in broadcast journalism from the renowned S.I. Newhouse School of Journalism at Syracuse University. Following graduation, AJ spent four seasons inside the giant baseball-shaped head of the New York Mets legendary mascot, Mr. Met. AJ's advice is currently sought after by fantasy sports owners from all over the globe. His innovative approach to statistical analysis has earned him high praise from colleagues and competitors alike and has made him a frequent guest of radio shows around the country. He lives with his wife and young son in Galloway, New Jersey.

Index